Raising Moms

Books by Rhonda H. Kelley
available from New Hope Publishers

"Woman's Guide" series

A Woman's Guide to Joyful Living
A Woman's Guide to Personal Discipline
A Woman's Guide to Servant Leadership
A Woman's Guide to True Contentment
A Woman's Guide to Personal Holiness
A Woman's Guide Spiritual Wellness

Raising Moms

Daughters Caring for Mothers in Their Later Years

By Rhonda H. Kelley

new
hope
PUBLISHERS

Birmingham, Alabama

New Hope® Publishers
P. O. Box 12065
Birmingham, AL 35202-2065
www.newhopepublishers.com

Library of Congress Cataloging-in-Publication Data

Kelley, Rhonda.
  Raising moms : daughters caring for mothers in their later years / by Rhonda H. Kelley.
  p. cm.
  ISBN 1-56309-992-6
  1. Daughters—Religious life. 2. Mothers and daughters—Religious aspects—Christianity. 3. Caring—Religious aspects—Christianity. I. Title.
  BV4551.3.K45 2006
  248.8'43—dc22
    2006001307

ISBN 1-56309-992-6

N064125 • 0406 • 5M1

Dedication

This work of love is dedicated to

my godly grandmothers,

Lupearl Compton and Ludie Harrington,

my godly mothers,

Joyce Harrington and Doris Kelley,

and my many spiritual mothers,

who have mentored me in faith and ministry.

—Rhonda Harrington Kelley
December 2005

Table of Contents

Foreword

Rhonda Harrington entered my life as a vivacious high school coed while my husband and I were students at New Orleans Baptist Theological Seminary. She participated in a pageant celebrating biblical womanhood, and, of course, she won! Some years later, our paths crossed again when she caught the eye of my brother and he won her hand in marriage. Rhonda brought to our family a wonderful heritage in godly disciplines of life and gracious hospitality in ministry—all woven through and through with unusual creativity and overflowing joy. During the passing of years, it became apparent that the human agent responsible for this marvelous package is Joyce Harrington, Rhonda's charming and gracious mother!

When the Lord placed Rhonda in the Kelley clan, He certainly knew what He was doing! Chuck, my only brother and now Rhonda's husband, experienced the investment of a loving and devoted mother also—one who fashioned his character and honed his giftedness with skill and determination. When Rhonda became Chuck's wife, she became a beloved daughter as well. Doris Kelley then took delight in passing along to her daughter-in-love many Kelley traditions—recipes, rituals, and examples of loving service. Rhonda was as surely a Kelley girl as were Dorothy Jean, Kathleen, Charlene, and Eileen, with all the rights and privileges, as well as responsibilities, that accompanied this familial role. Whatever the occasion, she rolled up her sleeves and attacked the task as would we all, for that is what being a family is all about.

The tapestries God weaves are indeed amazing, and what a mother pours into her daughter in training and mentoring is an investment that reaps unbelievable dividends when she begins to write checks on the deposits of love and grants of gracious and sacrificial living. The same is true for a mother-in-love and her daughter-in-love. When they embrace one another through the God-ordained union of families, they bond in the womb of sacrificial love and maternal joy. Their mutual respect and reciprocal service, not to mention the common love that brings them to a singular focus, are stronger than Super Glue and locked into place so that they can become forever friends, eternal kindred spirits, and unequivocally faithful colaborers. Yes, each has her own personality, strengths and weaknesses, unique giftedness, individual interests (as do all mothers and daughters), but they are also bound together by what they hold in common in family loyalty and devotion to those they love.

Raising Moms is not a book written in a vacuum but is one that arises from a precious true life experience you will find in "Rhonda's Story," which sets the scene for this entertaining and warm-hearted volume. You may see "the moms" as the heroines, and they are quite a dynamic duo! They have borne the burden in the heat of the day; they have paid their dues in rearing their own children and investing in the lives of countless others; they have served not only their families but their communities also—and they still do! They are women who deserve accolades and crowns and a return investment on all they have poured out in nurturing love and service over the years. That is exactly what God has given to them in Rhonda

Harrington Kelley, who is now their primary caregiver, social secretary, financial advisor, creative companion, and faithful friend and an exemplary heroine to us all. She can bring relief from anxiety to the moms, whatever the circumstances; she can prepare Papa for his date with Mom and put a sparkle in his one eye; and she gives me the perfect peace that my mom is enjoying her golden years to the maximum!

Yes, Rhonda is the clearinghouse for all of us as we delight in giving back to our moms just a bit of what they have given to us through the years. Rhonda covers not only the basics but also the serendipities. Her organizational skills, the resources she has uncovered, the challenges, and the rewards—all are covered with honesty and forthrightness. This book will not only be a treasure of memories for me because I know and love the moms, but its godly counsel and helpful resources will be a conduit of information to pass along to friends and students who are facing similar challenges of balancing quality care-giving with a myriad of other responsibilities.

May I add a note of thanks to Dr. Chuck Kelley, the esteemed president of New Orleans Baptist Theological Seminary, my alma mater, not only for finding Rhonda and bringing her into our family but also for making the personal sacrifices necessary to allow her to invest enormous amounts of time and creativity far beyond her responsibilities as the First Lady of NOBTS to oversee the care of the moms.

—Dorothy Kelley Patterson
Pecan Manor
Southwestern Baptist Theological Seminary
Fort Worth, Texas

Acknowledgments

I have often joked that I am a "high maintenance woman." While I laugh, I must admit that statement holds such truth. My daily life and ministry are dependent on the assistance of many others. I am so grateful for the help and support they give to me. I want to thank several people in particular for their help on this project, which has been in my heart for almost three years.

As always, I have experienced the power of the Holy Spirit. He has supernaturally worked in my life during this writing assignment, which was completed in the post-Katrina days. *Thank You, Lord!*

My husband of 32 years has been my constant source of confidence and strength. His many expressions of love throughout each day encourage and support me. His life is a living example of Christ to me and to so many others. He is not only the godly leader of New Orleans Baptist Theological Seminary but also the loving leader of our home. *Thank you, Chuck!*

My mother has been a lifelong influence on me. Her un-wavering commitment to the Lord and service to Him as well as her godly living have strengthened my faith and taught me about His grace. *Thank you, Mother!*

My mother-in-love has accepted me as her daughter and loved me unconditionally. Her devotion to the Lord and His church and her powerful prayer life are legacies of faith in my life and in the lives of each of her family members. *Thank you, Mom Kelley!*

My sister and her four precious boys add such joy to my life. Though our lives are very different, our love for each other is sure. My sister is always excited for me and interested in my experiences. *Thank you, Mitzi!*

Chuck's four sisters have loved me as a sister and supported me wholeheartedly as the primary caregiver of our parents. Each sister is involved personally in ministry and contributed significantly to this book. *Thank you, Dorothy, Kathy, Charlene, and Eileen!*

Members of our ministry team at the New Orleans Baptist Theological Seminary undergird all that I do in life and ministry. They manage the daily details so I can focus on God's call on my life. Many of the staff members support me, but several work directly with me and also care for our parents. *Thank you, Christian, Dee Dee, Janet, Jana, Trish, and Vanee!*

Many friends responded to a questionnaire for *Raising Moms* and shared their personal lessons about caregiving. I have learned so much from them and their parents. *Thank you, friends*, for giving of your time and letting me share your stories!

Thanks to each of you! I love and appreciate you. You have made *Raising Moms* a reality. I pray it will be a source of encouragement and help to others.

—Rhonda Harrington Kelley

Introduction

Rarely a day passes without the media addressing adult children caring for their aging parents. Newspaper headlines, magazine articles, and television features verify the increasing phenomena and offer guidance to caregivers. As baby boomers age, most find themselves balancing the demands of busy lives. They often juggle the responsibilities of raising their own children while providing care for their elderly parents. A recent congressional study concluded that women today will spend more time caring for their parents than they spent caring for their children. In fact, as the largest generation (baby boomers) approaches retirement age, a tidal wave of caregiving needs is developing. The population of seniors will more than double by 2050. Therefore, an even greater number of adult caregivers will be required in the future.

At the present time, about one fourth of US households (22 million) are already providing care for a relative or friend 50 years of age or older. The US Census Bureau predicts that by 2050, the percentage of Americans 65 years of age or older will grow to 21%. As many as 19 million senior adults will need some type of long-term professional care (*USA Today*, February 17, 2004). Many adult children will become caregivers for their aging parents; thus, it is important for adult children to understand the responsibilities of caregiving and the increasing needs of their parents.

Women are most often the primary caregivers. The nurturing nature of females equips them for caregiving. As mothers, they tenderly raised their children. As adult daughters, they will tenderly raise their parents—most often their mothers, because they tend to live longer than the fathers. Experts on aging do not like to promote role reversals, which may seem demeaning to the elderly, but in reality, adult children do become a parent figure to their parents. Raising parents, like raising children, is both a challenge and a blessing.

The purpose of this book is to provide information about the needs of senior adults and helpful hints to caregivers. Professional counsel and personal experiences are included to promote an aging parent's independence while ensuring adequate protection. Consideration is given to strengthening the mother-daughter relationship as well as to building family relationships and maintaining friendships. Biblical teachings are examined, and suggestions for church support are explored. Support systems are identified, yet the blessings of personally providing the care are emphasized.

This author's intent is to encourage individuals who are presently caring for their aging parents and to prepare all people facing a future of caregiving. Caregivers will be strengthened by the knowledge that others are experiencing similar challenges. Additional support is available from outside professional help, and for the Christian caregiver, supernatural power also is available from the Lord, who is glorified when His children care for one another. This book is meant to be read, reread, and then shared with a fellow caregiver.

Rhonda's Story

In recent years, I have found myself, like many of my contemporaries, facing both my own midlife challenges and the aging of my parents. My husband and I are now in a position of providing increasing support and care for my parents as well as his parents. While this reversal of roles is a precious privilege, it can often be a challenge. Together we seek God's direction in balancing the demands of our own lives while helping our parents with theirs.

Like most married couples, Chuck and I both are involved with our parents, but the primary responsibility for nurturing them is mine. I meet the daily needs of our parents, while my husband fulfills his responsibilities to his work. I make the daily phone calls, run errands, and spend more time with our parents. He is supportive of my role, is involved in the big decisions, and helps as needed. As a woman, daughter, and wife, I offer the nurturing that our mothers have always provided to us. I would never have dreamed that I would be so actively involved in the lives of both my mothers—my own mother and my mother-in-law. But I am, and it is a joy!

Chuck and I live in the city where I grew up and where my mother still lives. For most of my married life, I have lived only minutes away from my mother.

Three years ago, my husband's parents moved to New Orleans. Mr. Kelley was experiencing dementia and declining health, so he needed skilled nursing care. Since his needs are being met by the faithful nursing staff, my role in his care is mostly supportive. I have much more interaction with my precious mother-in-law, whom I call Mom Kelley.

Two years ago, my mother sold her home of many years and moved into the retirement setting where the Kelleys now live. It never occurred to me to pray for such a blessing: I have three parents living in one building. Lambeth House is a 12-story continued care facility. Mom Kelley lives independently in an apartment on the eleventh floor; my mother lives independently on the tenth floor, just below Mom Kelley; and Papa Kelley lives on the second floor in the skilled nursing center. So my visits are simple as I work my way down the elevator. God is so good!

It has been such a joy to spend time with our mothers. I lovingly call them "the moms." Chuck refers to our mothers fondly as "the golden girls." We have learned so much from our godly parents throughout our lives. Now we are entering a new chapter in our relationships with them. As our parents age, they have become more dependent on us. As they have faced health problems and lifestyle changes, they have sought our advice. In many ways, the roles have reversed. While it is a natural life progression, this stage has not come without some challenges. In God's providence, it has also brought some tender moments and precious experiences we will never forget. That is what I want to discuss with you in this book. God has taught me so much about honoring my parents, and they have taught me about godly living. It is time for me to share what I have learned about "raising moms" with others who will also provide care for their mothers entering their later years.

In this book, I have included personal insights as well as the life experiences of others. I have built a foundation on Scripture and added other helpful resources. In addition, I have attempted to provide factual information as well as practical suggestions. While I am not a medical professional, I am an experienced family member. The university of life is a great teacher!

It is my prayer that as you assume the responsibilities of caring for your mother, you will experience many blessings. I can honestly say that few experiences in my life have been as precious as this privilege of raising my moms!

Chapter One

Understanding Seniors

As the relationship between adult children and their parents develops through the years, it becomes very clear that parent and child are from two different generations, in more than a measure of time. Era of birth and experiences of life greatly impact values, decisions, and lifestyles. If adult children and their parents are to get along well, each must understand the generational differences of the other. While belief systems and personality types affect an individual's behavior, some general understanding about the generations may help the relationship. Often, a behavior or decision is typical of many people born at the same time in history, not just a unique idiosyncrasy of an individual. It helps to know your parent is not the only one to have those concerns, and you are not the only child to have those feelings.

I remember when I became acutely aware of these generational differences in our family. A couple of years ago, my sister-in-law Kathy, a school librarian living on a modest income, sent her parents money for food. She was concerned that they were running out of money because my mother-in-law had recently commented, "I don't have enough money to buy chicken this week." I had to laugh when I heard this because I had just met with Mom Kelley and their financial advisor. We had learned that the Kelleys were very well cared for financially. In fact, at that very moment, their checking account had a huge balance. I realized the impact of the Great Depression on my mother-in-law's thinking. They have abundant retirement savings, but because she is a member of the builder generation, she doesn't have the confidence that the money will always be available to her. Kathy now understands this fact and has not sent any other money to help her mother buy food.

Later my mother and sister had a similar encounter. After selling her home, my mother moved into a lovely retirement setting. Several months passed and my mother mentioned to my sister that she didn't have much money. My sister became concerned that Mother had moved into housing that required more money than she had available. Again, I was able to reassure my sister that Mother was financially secure. She, like others of her generation, talks like she is poor. Though she has adequate income and investments for her present lifestyle, Mother is always concerned that her money won't last. Because she lives frugally, Mother has always had the means to provide for herself. Again, the Great Depression and its sudden loss of wealth influenced her attitude about money.

A friend reported that her mother became angry at her because she bought a bunch of bananas without checking the price. Every penny is carefully counted by senior adults. We can certainly learn from the older generation how to be better stewards of our financial resources. We can also understand why the older generation is cautious about spending money.

It is very helpful for family members to consider generational differences as they relate to one another. Since the values, experiences, and goals of each generation vary, it is important to respect those differences. Tensions may develop between mothers and daughters who have different perspectives and priorities. Understanding and compromise is necessary as mother and daughter make important decisions. Support and encouragement of each value system can strengthen the relationship between mother and daughter.

If you have never considered the patterns of recent US generations, it might be productive for you to examine them now. While these are simply generalizations and may not always apply to every individual, they are helpful guidelines. Space doesn't allow a thorough review of each generation. Therefore, this chapter will present a summary of the generations, then address the builder and boomer generations particularly. Most senior mothers and their adult daughters today fall into those two age categories. Please read more about the generations in the resources cited or from the Barna Group (www.barna.org).

The Generations
Several important facts must be understood before beginning a discussion about the generations. These facts characterize the present culture:

- More people are alive today than at any other time in history.
- People are living longer lives than ever before.

- There are more senior adults living than ever before.
- When baby boomers reach 65 years of age, there will be more retired people than ever before.
- Options for senior adults are increasing dramatically.
- Families must prepare for the future so their aging parents will enjoy quality of life and greater independence.

Today the study of generational patterns is a field of its own. Publications and agencies provide information about each age group. Observations are recorded and research is compiled so that people can better understand the characteristics of the different generations. With increased knowledge, relationships across the generations can improve. Significant changes have been experienced in recent years as our society has moved from the modern to postmodern culture. Changing culture and generational differences affect who we are and what we expect in life.

The population of the United States has consistently grown through the years. The US Census 2004 estimation noted a record total population of 293,655,404. It is assumed that today's population is even greater. More than half (approximately 51%) of the people in America are female, and a growing number of residents are over 65 years of age. These statistics from the 2004 US Census are relevant to this discussion:

- 36,293,985 people are 65 years and over (12% of the total population)
- 61,952,636 people are 45 to 64 years (24% of the total population)
- 84,140,590 people are 25 to 44 years (29% of the total population)

While the senior population is larger than ever before in history, the future suggests additional growth of the oldest age group. With longer life comes a greater need for understanding between the generations.

The chart provided on the next page attempts to describe the generational differences. It is designed to summarize the descriptions, labels, influential members, characteristics, and influences of each generation alive at this time.

A quick glance at the characteristics of each age group summarized in the chart validates the change in influences, values, and motivations across the generations. If parents and children can accept their differences without criticism and understand each other's perspectives without condemnation, they will build healthier relationships. These generational differences, which are present throughout life, can become more apparent in later years as adult children assist their older parents. Conflict and tensions can be reduced if each family member accepts the other and understands the generational issues.

Seniors — The Builders

Most senior parents today are members of the builder generation, those born before 1946 who are in their sixties or older. Specific values and characteristics influence their thinking and decision making. According to Gary McIntosh, people in this age group are "connected by a place in time, by common boundaries, and by a common character" (*One Church, Four Generations*, page 15). Builders are described by Win and Charles Arn in their book *Live Long and Love It:* "We were here before panty hose, drip-dry clothes, ice makers, dishwashers, clothes dryers, freezers, and electric blankets" (page 6). Builders were also "born before the Pill, television, penicillin, polio shots, Frisbees, hula hoops, frozen foods, Dacron, Xerox, the Kinsey Report, radar, credit cards, ballpoint pens, tape decks, CDs, electric typewriters, and computers" (McIntosh, page 37). The oldest generation alive today has distinctive characteristics that influence how they live.

The Generations
A General Profile

GENERATIONS	Builders (<1946)	Boomers (1946–1964)	Busters (1965–1983)	Bridgers (1984–present)
DESCRIPTIONS	Get-it-done generation	Largest and most studied generation	Smallest generation	Newest generation
OTHER LABELS	G.I. generation Silent genera-tion	Leading-edge boomers Trailing-edge boomers	Bust Boomlet Generation X	Postmoderns
INFLUENTIAL MEMBERS	Bob Hope John F. Kennedy Ronald Reagan Billy Graham	Donald Trump Oprah Winfrey Sylvester Stallone Katie Couric Bill Clinton George W. Bush	Johnny Depp Julia Roberts Brooke Shields Greg Maddox	None yet identified
CHARACTERIS-TICS	Loyal Generous givers Fear being cast aside Powerful work ethic Frugal savers	Convenience Critical thinking Control Choices	Freedom Survival Neglect Practical education	Technologically astute Tolerant of diversity Fragmented preferences
INFLUENCES	World War I Roaring 20's Great Depression World War II Rural lifestyle Automobile Radio Airplane Korean War	Cold War Strong econo-my Vietnam War Civil rights movement Space race Television Education Rock and roll Energy crisis Watergate	Fluctuating economy Desert Storm MTV Video games High technology Berlin Wall dismantled AIDS	Volatile economy War on terror Internet Cell phones Personal digital assistants

Compiled from a variety of sources listed in the back of the book.

Let's look at several of these characteristics in respect to the mother-daughter relationship. Again, remember that these are generalizations about a group of people. Try to recognize those traits that apply to your loved one, so that your understanding will be strengthened and your cooperation enhanced.

The **loyalty** of seniors is a value to be admired. Most older adults are extremely loyal to organizations and people. That loyalty is often the catalyst for their commitment. As seniors age, they remain very committed to those groups they have joined and people they have known. When finances become fixed, they may still want to pay membership dues to organizations they can no longer attend, subscribe to professional publications though they no longer work, and telephone or write to friends that they have not seen in years. While continued involvement may be fueled by a reluctance to let go, it is also encouraged by a sense of loyalty and commitment.

I have a distinct memory of my maternal grandfather, a loyal Democrat, saying that he would vote for the Democratic candidate if it was "the devil himself." He was loyal! My husband and I see this trait of loyalty reflected in many ways in his mother. We smile when we remember his mother's loyalty to the Baylor University football team when we were in college. Mom Kelley would not leave the stadium until the buzzer sounded, and she remained confident that the Bears would win even if they were behind 50–0! She was a loyal fan.

As Papa Kelley's health has declined, she has been faced with many hard decisions. One hard decision was discontinuing subscriptions to Papa's professional organizations. It no longer seemed wise to spend the money for his airplane journals when he was no longer able fly his plane. But, out of loyalty, she continued the subscriptions for years. However, it is definitely worth every penny Mom Kelley spends on long distance phone calls, greeting cards, and postal stamps to keep in touch with her friends in Texas. She is a committed, loyal friend. Children must understand their parents' strong sense of loyalty even when personal commitment is not as important today. Children must be patient with parents who are making difficult life decisions. In fact, Chuck and I laugh as we recall a time when in frustration Mom Kelley told my husband, the president of a large Southern Baptist Seminary—"You don't have to make hard decisions! Only 80-year-olds have to make hard decisions!"

Seniors are also **generous givers**. While boomers are usually self-focused, builders consider the needs of others and give accordingly. Seniors will sacrifice personally to help others who are in need financially. Even on a fixed income, the older generation receives great joy in giving to others. Daughters must understand this characteristic of the builder generation and not be worried when parents seem to give away too much money. Their generosity is to be admired. Caution must also be practiced so that generous seniors are not taken advantage of by self-serving people or family members.

My husband relates the sad story of a Christian man's scholarship endowment to the seminary being rescinded by his children after his death. While he wanted to give generously to the Lord's work, his children were focused on their own welfare. In different ways, we have also seen generosity displayed in the giving of our own parents. Chuck's mother has such a generous nature. She often writes checks to those having financial need while withdrawing from her savings to cover her own monthly expenses. My mother loves to give to the Lord's work. She often laments that she doesn't have more money to give to the church and the seminary. However, she gives sacrificially. Seniors truly enjoy giving generously to others more than keeping money for themselves. The children of these generous givers should learn the joy of giving and become less selfish with their own money.

Seniors often **fear being cast aside**. They are concerned that they will lose meaning and purpose in their lives as they grow older. They believe they have little to offer their well-educated offspring. Quality of life is important to them. Thus, parents who are aging may express their concern about insignificance to their children. Daughters should demonstrate empathy to mothers who feel that they are becoming a burden rather than a blessing. Tenderly, daughters can assure their mothers that they are of great worth and value.

I have often heard older women say, "I have nothing to offer." When younger women attempt to develop mentoring relationships, seniors seem intimidated by the abilities of the younger generation and overlook the importance of their own life experiences. If younger women recognize this tendency of older women to demean themselves, they can encourage older women to share what they have learned with those younger. Younger women can help dispel the fear of being cast aside that many seniors may feel. Women's groups in churches can encourage the sharing of life experiences through mentoring programs.

It has been such a blessing to see how many seniors gain new meaning in life through the Senior Adult Mission Lab at our seminary. Church groups bring their seniors to New Orleans to stay on campus and minister in the city. They enjoy the food and sights of this great world city while being involved in hands-on ministry. Hours are spent feeding the homeless, helping drug addicts, and caring for the young on the streets. Many older adults have gained greater significance in their own lives while ministering to others through Mission Lab. Seniors can be used by God in a mighty way to minister to others, and their sense of significance can be strengthened.

The builder generation also has a **powerful work ethic**. They have worked hard all their lives and want to keep on working. On the other hand, many of their children have been given everything on a silver platter. Younger generations have come to expect abundance without work. Younger people can learn how to work hard from parents who continue to work tirelessly. Tensions may develop when older parents criticize the lack of effort in children or the children judge the parents' hard work as unnecessary.

Almetta Wilson is 75 years old and has worked at the New Orleans Baptist Theological Seminary for 45 years. She has helped with 88 graduation receptions in the President's Home. She has an amazing work ethic. She chooses not to retire because work is her life. She works tirelessly while other younger workers wear out. Ms. Almetta doesn't understand why young people today are so lazy. Her expectations for those she supervises are much greater than they desire. These traits reflect the dramatic differences between the powerful work ethic of the older generation and the less diligent work ethic of the younger generations.

There are many other characteristics that describe the builder or senior generation. While they may also influence the relationship between mother and daughter, these four seem to have profound impact: loyalty, generosity, fear of being cast aside, and powerful work ethic. It is helpful to recognize and respect these values. Now let's examine several traits of the baby boomer generation that may impact the mother-daughter relationship.

Adult Children — The Boomers

Many adults entering midlife are balancing the responsibilities of demanding careers, growing families, and aging parents. This group, often called "the sandwich generation," is typically in the boomer generation, those born between 1946 and 1964. It would be helpful to recognize common characteristics of this younger generation as well as traits of their parents' older generation in order to increase understanding and decrease stress.

Boomers as a generation value **convenience**. Microwaves, take-out food, and drip-dry clothes have made lives easier for most daughters. Decisions are often made because of convenience—closest churches, simplest routines, or easiest recipes. Mothers have trouble understanding a busy daughter's many conveniences. As the adult daughter juggles work and home, business and family, she must rely upon modern conveniences. It is the only way she can get it all done. The busy lives of most daughters qualify them for the "Superwoman" title.

I am a certified baby boomer, born in 1951 and characterized by many of these generational traits. I am a self-confessed woman of convenience. Yes, I am a high-maintenance woman. It takes many people and many gadgets to help me live my fast-paced life. I definitely believe I should support the economy and affirm the skills of others by buying ready-to-eat foods. My mother jokingly calls me "the mistress of prepared foods." I warm up meals and often eat out. I love my tea towel that says, "For dinner I have made reservations." Yes, I love shortcuts. And I do know the grocery stores in town with the best prepared foods.

Early in our marriage, I learned to ask for help when I entertained. Chuck and I love to get together for meals with friends, but I cannot entertain by myself with such a busy schedule. I often have potluck dinners for friends rather than doing all the cooking myself. Now I invite a faculty wife to help me hostess meals in our home. It all boils down to convenience. I also demonstrate my need for convenience with my mother-in-law. While I willingly run errands for her, I encourage her to let me know her needs as soon as possible so I can work her errands into my daily routine. We boomers love our conveniences and we are bound by our schedules. When mother and daughter recognize these tendencies, both can be satisfied.

Critical thinking is also a characteristic of the baby boomer generation. The most educated of all generations, boomers seek knowledge and information to make decisions. Data is carefully analyzed while lists of positives and negatives are compiled. Boomers have become hypercritical thinkers. Many boomers spend years in school and are considered professional students by their parents. Education seems essential to decision making. The tendency of children to ruminate over even small matters may seem confusing to senior parents. However, critical thinking is a hallmark of the boomer generation.

Chuck and I wrote dissertations at the same time and received our doctoral degrees the same year. Between us, we have 50 years of formal education. Our families thought we would never get out of school. When I finished my degree and earned the title "Doctor," I was eager to tell my grandfather. Pop quickly responded, "Some kind of doctor you are—can't help if I am sick and won't make much money." Though he was proud of my accomplishment, my grandfather was wiser than his seventh-grade education.

When the time came for the Kelleys to find alternative living arrangements, Chuck and I jumped into our boomer thinking mode. We researched by visiting 16 facilities in Dallas and New Orleans. We carefully compiled pertinent information, summarizing the advantages and disadvantages of each facility. Of course, Mom Kelley was overwhelmed by this life-changing event as well as the influx of new information. However, she is also not a member of our critical thinking generation. It did help her to have facts in writing to guide her decision making. When making the living arrangement decision, our tendency to ponder was a plus. Chuck and I did have to be careful not to overwhelm her with too much information at one time. We thrived on the abundance of data, though she was threatened by it. Parents and children can learn from each other if the strengths of their generations are appreciated.

Baby boomers also need **control**. Strong-willed, driven, successful, opinionated adult children may want to take control of everything, including the lives of their parents. Because of professional success, boomers are often in charge of their businesses. Their strong leadership styles may interfere with their family relationships. At a time when aging parents must let go of some control in their lives, aggressive children may try to take control. It is a fine line, a delicate balance in a mother-daughter relationship between control and free will, dependence and independence. Again, both mother and daughter will benefit if the strengths and weaknesses of control are recognized.

I am a strong personality by nature. My mother tells me, "You came out of the womb in charge of the world!" And I often think that the world would be a better place if I *was* in charge of it. My mother and I are working on this balance in our relationship. While I do want to offer her support and assistance, I must not try to control her life. While she does need my help at times, Mother wants to be totally independent. She seems to love it when I chauffeur her around, but at times she responds defensively when I offer to pick her up. Since she is still healthy and active, control is not a significant issue. However, we need to be ready to balance the power of control when the time comes. Mother recently told a friend that she used to keep me at arm's length, but now she is letting me get closer to her. We are trying to balance my desire for support and her need for independence.

My mother-in-law does not seem bothered by my take-charge manner. In fact, she has become quite dependent on me to help her make decisions. She often calls me her "brain" and depends on me to remember information for her. I suggest that it may be easier for women to relinquish control to their in-laws than to their own blood relative. I often find it easier to make suggestions to my mother-in-law than to my own mother. While Mom Kelley readily accepts my advice, Mother is more resistant. It is probably because I make gentle suggestions to my mother-in-law, but give forceful advice to my mother. I also see this different dynamic with my sisters-in-law. Chuck's four sisters tend to tell their mother what to do—go to the doctor, buy a new dress, come for a visit, etc. On the other hand, I try to listen to her as she expresses her desires, then facilitate her wishes. I need to learn to do that with my own mother and resist the desire to control. In general, baby boomers like to exercise control. At times this strength becomes a weakness.

Boomers also expect a wide range of **choices**. For parents, life may have been simpler—Ford made automobiles, Coke was the only soft drink, and SAS made the only comfortable shoes. However, their boomer children have always had an array of choices—many automobile companies and models, different soft drink companies and flavors, and an abundance of designers of comfortable shoes. Talk about varied choices—my husband loves to drink Diet Cherry Vanilla Dr. Pepper. That many different flavors in one drink seems overstimulating to me, but they offer variety to him. Therefore, while seniors are content with the same brand of detergent, their children purchase a cleaner for every type of clothing. Choices are routine for boomers but overwhelming for seniors. Daughters can help their mothers cope with the many choices of life.

On a recent airplane trip with my mother, Chuck introduced her to the iPod. At first she was intimidated by the technology, then her curiosity got the best of her. She even decided to listen to Chuck's iPod with his Bose headphones. Initially, she listened to what he selected because she could not conceive of over 500 CDs on the tiny electronic device. However, later she searched for songs she knew. Multiple stations, many options, maximum choices are expected by boomers, while builders enjoy the simple things of life. Yes, times have changed and younger people seem to accept change with greater ease than their parents. A recent email reminded me of the impact of such changes in our lives today. You know you live in 2005 if…

- You accidentally enter your password on the microwave.
- You haven't played solitaire with real cards in years.
- You have a list of 15 phone numbers to reach your family of three.
- Your reason for not staying in touch with friends is that they don't have email addresses.
- When you go home after a long day at work, you still answer the phone in a business manner.
- When you make phone calls from home, you accidentally dial "9" to get an outside line.

These and many other changes challenge seniors. Adult children can help the older generation manage the impact of change. Daughters can bridge the gap between the generations. The term "generation gap" is often used to describe the differences between those of varied age groups. A gap or division is natural when people who were born during different times and who have experienced different events interact. A generation gap develops because each generation reacts in a different way to the same event. Relationships with people of different ages are a part of life. Therefore, it is necessary for everyone to understand the generations so that relationships can be healthy and not unhealthy. Though of the same gender, mother and daughter are of different generations. Love, acceptance, and understanding are needed by both to promote personal fulfillment and proper care as the years progress.

Mother-Daughter Reflections

1. What challenges have you and your mother experienced in trying to understand each other's generational differences?

2. Which trends among the builder generation are reflected in your parents?

3. Which trends among the boomer generation are most reflected in you?

4. Discuss these generational differences with your parents, and try to learn from each other.

5. What changes will you make to adjust to your mother's generational style?

Chapter Two

The Mother-Daughter Relationship

No human relationship is any stronger, deeper, or longer lasting than the relationship between mother and daughter. Before birth, the bond develops as a mother nurtures and cares for her daughter inside the womb. At birth, the mother-daughter bond is strengthened by the miracle of new life and the biological similarities of females. After birth, the unique connection between mother and daughter continues through the life stages and throughout many life experiences. In good times and bad, a mother's unconditional love supports and guides her child. A daughter's devotion typically withstands teenage rebellion and young adult independence. The mother and daughter relationship is truly a special gift from God—one to last for a lifetime and to be passed along as a treasured legacy.

In a recent newspaper article, a native of New Orleans reflected on her life as a nurse in World War II and her role as a mother. Her military service was eventful since she participated in the Normandy invasion and was captured by Nazi troops. After the war, she was released and returned home. She married and had ten children. When she was age 84, one of her children asked her which was more difficult, raising ten children or the battle for the Ardennes. Rosalou Freeland Etue answered, "Well, the war ended" (*The New Orleans Times–Picayune*, August 14, 2005). How true! Parenting and the mother-daughter relationship are unending. Therefore, it is essential to caregiving for both mother and daughter to understand this unique relationship.

The Creator's Design

Woman was created by God and women continue to be unique creations of God. After He created the heavens and the earth, the light and the dark, the water and the land, the sun and the moon, the fish and the birds, God created man (Genesis 1). God made man in His own image and for His own pleasure. Then, God determined that "It is not good for the man to be alone" (Genesis 2:18*a*). So God created woman from the rib of man. God made for man "a helper who is like him" (Genesis 2:18*b*). He called the helper "woman" because she was taken out of man (Genesis 2:21–23). He gave both of them special assignments: man to name the animals and woman to help the man. Then God placed man and woman together in the Garden of Eden, to be united together as one—two unique creations, equal in worth and value, different in role and function, complementing each other in other in marriage and life.

From the beginning, God created woman to be unique. Thus, women are different from men—physically, mentally, emotionally, and socially. Therefore, mothers and their daughters have a special relationship because of their gender. Their feminine nature connects them from birth throughout life. Let's examine what the Bible teaches about women so we can better understand the mother-daughter relationship.

Women are created by God. The knowledge that God is Creator gives women value and worth. Mothers and daughters can each have a strong sense of self-worth and healthy self-esteem because they are each created by God and loved by Him. Mother and daughter are equal in the eyes of God and both are esteemed by Him. Genesis 1:27 says, "So God created man in His own image; He created him in the image of God; He created them male and female." Women, like men, were blessed by God (Genesis 1:28). Mothers and daughters today receive the blessings of God. One should not be jealous of the other's attributes or abilities since both are created in the image of God.

Women are created female. God created two different types of human beings—male and female (Genesis 1:27). He did not create only one gender, but two specific genders. Woman was not an afterthought. She was a part of God's creative plan to complete and complement man: "It is not good for the man to be alone. I will make a helper who is like him" (Genesis 2:18). God gave woman a feminine nature that would correspond perfectly to the male nature. Woman was not created by man, designed by herself, nor shaped by the culture. Woman was created female by God as a part of His divine plan.

Women are given a specific task. God created woman because man needed a helper. In the Bible, the role of "helper" (Hebrew *ezer*) is a position of great honor. God identified

Himself as a "helper" in Exodus 18:4 and Deuteronomy 33:7, and Jesus later called the Holy Spirit "Helper" (John 14:16; 15:26 NKJV). Woman was given a specific identity when she was created by God as a helper, one who walks alongside and gives assistance. Thus, women today who accept this biblical pattern of womanhood fulfill their roles as helpers in all their relationships. Nurturing is a natural trait of women because of this God-given task.

On my business cards from the New Orleans Baptist Theological Seminary, my title is described as "President's Wife." Often when I give my card to women, they question that title and suggest I should list titles I have earned in my own right. This is my response to them without apology or hesitation: "My most important role in life is to support my husband in his ministry." Yes, I have an earned PhD degree. Yes, I am a trustee-elected Professor of Women's Ministry at the seminary. And yes, I am a published author of many books and a frequent Christian speaker for women's groups. But the greatest calling in my life is to be the wife of Chuck Kelley. God's plan for my life is to be my husband's helper. Together we complement and complete each other. We are stronger together as a couple than either of us would be alone. God's plan is perfect. While both of us are created in His image and both have great worth in His eyes, our roles in marriage are different. Chuck is the loving leader in our home and I am his helper, willingly submitting to his position of authority in our home (Ephesians 5:22–33; 1 Peter 3:1–7). Our godly marriage is a testimony of God's perfect plan for the marital union.

Because of God's divine plan, mothers and daughters share the same creative design. Mothers can nurture the feminine nature of their daughters, and daughters can follow the godly example of their mothers. The gender bond between mother and daughter is very strong and continues throughout life.

The Mother's Influence

A mother naturally has a close bond with the children she has birthed and raised. Mothers also have tremendous influence on the lives of their children. From birth, mothers, both biological and adoptive, typically spend more time with their children than fathers or others do. Thus, by actions and words, mothers shape the characters of their children over time. One example of the mother's influence is often heard on television when a professional athlete in a media interview shouts out, "Hi, Mom!" Many children today would identify their mother as the most influential person in their lives. The influence of mothers on their children is universal and powerful.

In addition to character development, godly mothers have a profound influence on the spiritual development of their children. Motherhood is a high calling of God and it is an all-consuming task. No greater effort is expended in life than raising children. The work is full-time and lasts for a lifetime, but the influence is great. Mothers who teach the Scriptures to their children diligently and walk in God's way continually can be confident of their godly influence (Deuteronomy 6:6–7). The issue is not whether mothers will have influence on their children, but whether their influence will be positive or negative.

My mother has had a profound influence on my sister and me. We will never fully understand the many ways she has shaped and molded us. Though my sister and I jokingly confess that "we have become our mother," we aspire to be like her in many ways. Mother's influence on us is ongoing, though our relationship has changed over time. It is still difficult for Mother to let go and not tell us what to do. She has to resist trying to raise my sister's sons. We often remind her, "You are the grandmother, not the mother!" Though her role has changed, Mother continues to have powerful influence on our lives.

The Bible contains numerous examples of godly mothers who influenced their children positively. Hannah was devoted to her son, yet willingly offered him to the Lord (1 Samuel 1:27–28). Her faithful life was a godly example to Samuel, who was used by God in a mighty way. The Canaanite woman demonstrated great faith when she sought help from Jesus for her demon-possessed daughter (Matthew 15:21–28; Mark 7:24–30). Her godly life was a testimony not only to her daughter but to others. A mother's living faith can provide a profound influence on her children.

While many mothers in the Bible provide godly influences on their children, other mothers in the Bible have ungodly influence. Athaliah, the idolatrous mother of King Ahaziah, guided her son into evil (2 Kings 8:26–27). Gomer, the immoral wife of the prophet Hosea, led their daughters into sin (Hosea 2:4). The cycle of negative influence in the Bible and the world today can be changed with the help of the Lord. While ungodly mothers do impact their children, God can redeem the relationship for His good.

The lifestyles of mothers can greatly influence their children. Because of their feminine natures, mothers can have profound, life-changing influence on their daughters. Mothers and daughters naturally have a special bond because they are the same gender. However, because of the gender bond, competition between them can often develop. In her book *Aging Mothers and Their Adult Daughters*, Karen Fingerman reported that despite conflicts and complicated emotions, the mother-daughter bond is so strong that 80% to 90% of women at midlife report good relationships with their mothers.

Some conflicts exist throughout the relationship. Unconsciously, mothers want daughters to be like them, have their same priorities, and pursue their same goals. Mothers may pressure their daughters to follow exactly in their footsteps.

Daughters may feel the pressure and experience guilt. If mothers and daughters recognize this natural tendency, they can avoid inevitable conflict. Acceptance of each other is the key to a healthy relationship. Sheehan and Donorfio discussed the unique relationship between mothers and daughters in their article, "Efforts to Create Meaning in the Relationship Between Aging Mothers and Their Caregiving Daughters," published recently in the *Journal of Aging Studies*.

I remember clearly my mother's reaction when she learned my husband and I were unable to have children. While Chuck and I had a peace from God about our infertility, my mother seemed hurt. While her reaction at first surprised me, I later realized her disappointment was a result of her love for me. She loved being a mother, and she had always assumed that I would be a mother, too. By not having children, I was unable to follow in her footsteps of motherhood and would miss out on some of her most precious blessings. Over the years, our relationship has grown. Her influence on my life has been profound even though I have never had my own children.

The Daughter's Relationship

From birth, a daughter has a special relationship with her mother. Her relationship is based on a biological need that continues throughout her life. The basic need is for nurture. The mother nurtures the daughter, the daughter nurtures the mother, and both nurture others. The nurturing nature of women is a part of God's human design. Therefore, the mother-daughter bond may become the closest, most all-consuming, compassionate relationship women will ever experience. Gina Shaw concluded that "no relationship is quite as primal as the one between a mother and her daughter" (*Discovery Health*).

In her book *Mother-Daughter Wisdom: Creating a Legacy of Physical and Emotional Health*, Dr. Christiane Northrup suggests that human mothers are much like the most dangerous beast in the forest—the mother bear who ferociously protects her young. A mother unselfishly cares for her child and courageously protects her child. The daughter is always aware of her mother's devotion though her understanding seems to increase when she herself has a child. Mothers and their adult daughters form even deeper bonds as both develop their nurturing natures. Karen Fingerman found that "mother-daughter relationships take on different characteristics at different stages of life" (*Aging Mothers and Their Adult Daughters*).

A daughter's relationship with her mother experiences significant changes through the years. In infancy, the daughter is totally dependent upon her mother. In childhood, the daughter separates from her mother, developing some independence. In adolescence, the daughter distances herself from her mother, often developing an air of superiority. In adulthood, the daughter typically resumes a closer relationship with her mother. Their goals and interests are more similar. And in later years, the middle-aged adult daughter often becomes the mother as her mother begins to age.

I have certainly seen the relationship with my mother develop through the years. While we have always had a healthy relationship, we are even closer today. We enjoy spending time together and have similar interests. I often call Mother just to talk and she calls me for advice. Our parent-child relationship has developed into friendship through the years. In fact, over time we even share more physical traits and similar mannerisms. People often comment about our look-alike appearance. It has been a joy to experience our special bond.

The In-Law Relationship

It is important to mention the relationship between a daughter and her mother-in-law. The Christian wife should strive to develop a healthy relationship with her husband's mother. Many people find the in-law relationship is often rocky, and thus it is the brunt of many jokes. Many women report a difficult relationship with their mother-in-law, which can escalate through the years. The mother-in-law/daughter-in-law relationship is often more challenging since these women come from different backgrounds, are from different generations, and live different lifestyles. Though they love the same man, these women may have difficulty loving each other. A mother-in-law and daughter-in-law need not be best friends, but they must have a cordial relationship. Even if they do not necessarily *like* each other, they must *love* each other. Later in life, the wife may be needed to care for her husband's aging parents. A loving relationship provides tremendous support as the years progress.

The Bible records many relationships created by marriage. In Hebrew society, the husband and wife were more closely associated with the groom's parents than the bride's. The bride left her family to become a member of her husband's family. Some family relationships in the Bible were hostile. Isaac and Rebekah had estranged relationships with Esau and his wives (Genesis 26:34–35). However, many family relationships were loving. Ruth's strong bond with her mother-in-law, Naomi, is a godly example to women today.

Christian wives today should love and respect their mother-in-law. Likewise, mothers-in-law should support and encourage their daughters-in-law. While wives today maintain close kinships with their own family, they must also embrace their husband's family. These women can strengthen the family if they will build loving relationships. Both can contribute to the spiritual legacy of the family (Psalm 78:4–6).

Our friend Carol Ann had the privilege of caring for her mother-in-law in her home for many years. She recalls the blessings of togetherness and some challenges of sharing the kitchen. Over the years, the ladies developed a great relationship. In fact, Carol Ann said that if she and Jimmy ever had a fight, her mother-in-law would side with her! (Chuck says that about his mother and me, too!) Carol Ann related the cutest story about her sweet and very proper mother-in-law.

> On a cold winter day while we were out of town, Grandmother went out to the mailbox in her gown, robe, and crochet house shoes. Suddenly, the door behind her slammed shut and was locked. Not knowing what to do and already shivering, Grandmother went to the house next door where a retired minister and his wife lived. They invited her in their home for breakfast. We returned before long and Grandmother came back home. We laughed for years about her early morning visitation in her nightie!

How wonderful to see mother-in-law and daughter-in-law love each other so dearly and enjoy each other so immensely!

I am so blessed with godly in-laws. My husband's parents have accepted me and loved me from the beginning of our marriage. In recent years, my mother-in-law and I have developed an even closer relationship since they now live in New Orleans. She is my prayer warrior and loves to introduce me to her friends as her "daughter-in-love," not daughter-in-law. I am grateful for our loving relationship. Recently a friend of hers commented that I was a daughter-in-law and not a daughter. Mom Kelley quickly corrected her!

All mother-daughter relationships are important. Begin today to nurture love and affection for your mother. Also, if you are married, kindle a loving relationship with your mother-in-law. You can do so as you remember that God created you, your mother, and your husband's mother in His image. Your mothers have profound influence on your life, and you should have a great appreciation for them.

The mother-daughter relationship is unique and should be appreciated. A healthy mother-daughter relationship in earlier years will promote a happier mother-daughter relationship in later years. No matter the current emotional state of that relationship, it is never too late for mothers and daughters to cultivate a good one. The two women can strengthen each other, support each other, and satisfy each other as the years pass.

Mother-Daughter Reflections

1. Do you believe you were created by God in His own image? Read Genesis 1:26–2:7 to affirm your worth and value in the eyes of God. How does being created by God in His image influence your thoughts about yourself?

2. What influence has your mother had on your life? If you are a mother, what influence do you want to have on your children? Ask the Lord to give you godly influence.

3. What is your relationship with your mother? If there are tensions between you, seek forgiveness from God and let Him restore your relationship.

4. If you have a daughter, what is your relationship with her? Seek to build your relationship on love, trust, and friendship.

5. If you are married, what is your relationship with your mother-in-law? Try to develop a supportive, encouraging, mutually beneficial relationship.

Chapter Three

Dealing with Decline

P arents often find it hard to see their children grow up—to start to school, begin to drive, leave home for college, and get married. They go through a process of letting go as the child gradually becomes an independent adult. On the other end of the spectrum, it is difficult for children to watch their parents age. The child watches as parents retire, experience health challenges, stop driving, and face death. It is difficult for the child also to let go as the parents decline and become more dependent. Though difficult, it is a part of God's plan—the cycle of life.

The aging of parents is a challenging transition for most children. Many times our natural response is to ignore the fact of our parents' aging. In the same way a person jokes about age or denies a birthday, children may want to pretend that their parents aren't aging. That illusion can continue as long as parents are thriving. But for many, a health crisis, milestone birthday, or decision about living arrangements may force a look at reality. The truth must be accepted—time is marching on and all people age. The choice then focuses on how to respond to the inevitable aging of a loved one.

Though adults are living longer and more productive lives today, everyone ages. Parents may live many more years, but their decline is inevitable. Adult children must be aware of subtle changes in function and offer support as needed. Dialogue between parents and children about the future care of parents should take place long before the decisions are necessary. Because aging is a gradual process, the family typically has time to consider options. It is helpful to all family members if decline can be handled proactively and not reactively. If plans are made in advance and not in an emergency, multiple options can be considered and careful planning can be made.

As years pass, each person can expect to face decline. Decline is experienced in different ways and to different degrees by every person. A knowledge of family history and accumulated information from personal health history can help people prepare for their own gradual declines. However, since only God knows the future, mortal human beings are never fully prepared for their own decline or the decline of those they love. Human decline that is a part of normal aging usually involves a decrease in physical, mental, and social functioning. This chapter will briefly address each area of decline to provide assistance for those children who are caring for their aging parents.

Physical Decline

Aging parents experience many different physical challenges. Some older people face the typical health changes while others develop medical problems. Some health problems are chronic (long-term, persistent) while others are acute (short-term, transient). Each health challenge can be debilitating to an elderly person. The physical problems may require family support as well as medical attention. As a result, children become increasingly involved in their parents' health care in later years. Information and participation are important as parents experience physical decline.

One of the first health decisions is the choice of a physician. It is important to the parents and children that a primary care doctor be reliable and readily available. While general medical training may be adequate, it is helpful for the doctor to be experienced in elder care. The medical field today has a specialization called gerontology—medical specialists who care primarily for older patients. Gerontologists are experienced in long-term care of the elderly. Families may gain additional support from the services of a gerontologist who can assist with present medical needs and anticipate future challenges.

It is natural for a senior adult to experience gradual physical decline. Mobility problems are common among seniors due to arthritis, heart problems, or other conditions. Seniors often are weak and have difficulty walking far distances. Others have balance problems and must walk with assistance. Some seniors are best transported in a wheelchair. Regulations for handicapped access today are very helpful. Many senior adults can utilize handicapped parking stickers, walking sticks, walkers, and personalized wheelchairs. However, children must often seek the mobility assistance their proud parents refuse. My sweet husband must frequently remind his mother to use her walking stick. While she is not thrilled to use it, Mom Kelley is aware of how much it helps her when she follows her son's wise counsel. We have also made decisions about the wheelchair purchase for Papa Kelley as he has needed physical support. Professionals have been helpful in securing the needed equipment.

Over time, the basic senses also diminish—vision, hearing, smell, taste, and touch may be less sensitive. Most seniors lose accuracy in their vision, others develop glaucoma, and some have cataracts. Regular vision examinations are important. Hearing problems may develop. Audiology evaluations can detect hearing loss. Many senior adults benefit from hearing aids fitted to their particular auditory losses. While many seniors resist hearing aids, they must understand that significant gains have been made in hearing aid technology to improve appearance, fit, and function. Other sensory loss should be monitored by the physician. Medical interventions may help slow the decline or compensate for the loss.

Many of my friends who are caring for their parents report resistance to hearing aids. Mothers may vainly deny their need for hearing aids or simply not want to struggle with them. One friend sought help from her mother's doctor and was a bit frustrated by the lack of professional support. She wondered: "How can doctors help us convince our parents that hearing aids provide improved quality of life? I talked with my mother about hearing aids until I was blue in the face. She stubbornly refused and missed out on verbal interaction with her family and friends. I am convinced that Mother would have worn hearing aids if the doctor had told her to. We need doctors to make firm recommendations and support us as we try to help our parents."

Hearing a conversation on the telephone becomes increasingly difficult for older people. Numerous assistive devices have been developed to amplify sound on the telephone. Dr. Susan Vogel, who cares for Chuck's parents, made a very helpful recommendation for amplifying telephone volume. She purchased an inexpensive hearing assistive device from a local electronics store for her father. He benefited from the headphone and amplifier. She has now purchased two of the hearing devices for the geriatric unit at the hospital where she practices. Technology can assist your loved ones in practical ways as they face physical decline.

Older adults can develop many different diseases. Because this is not a medical book nor is it written by a medical professional, specific illnesses will not be discussed. However, it is important to obtain an accurate diagnosis, gather relevant information, and seek appropriate treatment of your parent's illness. Many advances have been made in medicine and many illnesses can be treated effectively. As you become more involved in your parents' care, you will learn about their specific health conditions and can assist them in medical decisions. While there is not much that adult children can do to change the health of their parents, there are some guidelines to follow. Encourage your parents to take good care of themselves and be proactive in their care.

1. Regular physical checkups are important for early detection of medical problems as well as ongoing management of health needs. Many senior adults have an aversion to doctors and hospitals. They avoid medical help until an emergency develops. Unlike the younger generation, older parents often feel doctors are only for the sick. You may need to convince them of the importance of regular checkups. The doctor can often reinforce this practice by recommending follow-ups at specific intervals or in a specific period of time. Developing a regular routine for doctor visits is a helpful practice.

My mother-in-law has never gone to the doctor regularly. In fact, she believes that doctors are a last resort. Since she has moved to New Orleans and I began assisting with her care, I have encouraged her to see the doctor regularly. Regular checkups have always been a priority in my life. I am grateful for my mother's insistence on annual physicals. Though my mother-in-law still protests that it is a waste of my time and the doctor's time, she has gone to the doctor regularly and has as a result experienced better health. Now she knows that she will see her primary care doctor once a year, her optometrist every three months, and her urologist every three months. That's our medical routine.

2. Consistent intake of prescribed medication is critical. Many senior adults forget to take their prescribed medicine, or they may take their medicine too often. The daily pill containers can help regulate medicine. It may be helpful to get two containers—one for daytime and one for nighttime. Label them and help your parents develop a routine for organizing their pills and taking them. Sometimes senior adults discontinue their medication because of the high cost of prescriptive drugs. Monitor their medicines and get financial assistance when possible.

My mother recently confessed that she had forgotten to take her pills one morning. She noticed that she felt tired and uncomfortable during the day. The next morning she realized her error. Her pills for the previous day were still in her daily pill box. While she was frustrated with herself for forgetting her pills, I was grateful that she had a system for her medicine. And I doubt that she will make that mistake again.

3. Proper nutrition is always important to health, but especially during the later years. Talk with your parents about their eating habits. Ensure that they eat one balanced meal each day. Take them out to eat or cook for them often to guarantee their good nutrition. Help them follow prescribed diets for health problems and observe any significant changes in weight. Good nutrition is always important, but it is even more essential in the later years.

Papa Kelley has always loved to eat. In his last few years, he has become fixated on sweets—cookies, cakes, ice cream. While we want him to be happy and often indulge his pleasures, it is necessary for him to eat a healthy diet. His daily intake is carefully monitored by his skilled nursing staff as well as his wife of 63 years. Recently Papa became sick and his appetite decreased. We became concerned as he lost weight. How grateful we are now as his infection has cleared and his appetite has returned! At his recent 85th birthday party, he ate everything in his reach—his sandwiches, cake, and ice cream, plus anyone else's he could get his hands on. One of the greatest benefits of a health care facility is a dietary staff who will carefully monitor each patient's nutritional needs.

My mother and I often talk about healthy eating. Both of us have high cholesterol thanks to our family genetics and our love for food (not to mention the delicious cuisine in New Orleans!). I try to encourage her to watch her diet and exercise regularly. Mother encourages me as well. A recent checkup found Mother's cholesterol to be high again. She confessed to me that she had started putting chocolate syrup in her skim milk to make it taste better! We laughed as she decided it would just be better for her to drink whole milk or get used to the flavor of the skim milk. I guess I need to *continue* encouraging her to eat a healthy diet.

4. Regular exercise and daily activity is essential to good health and quality of life. Some appropriate form of exercise or activity can be practiced by every person. Exercise is good for the body and the soul. It strengthens the organs and muscles as well as stimulates the mind. Some exercise or movement every day is important to every person who is physically able. It seems that fitness is a greater concern to people today.

My mother is enjoying exercise regularly for the first time in her life. She has always tried to exercise, but has often failed since it was inconvenient. Because her retirement facility has a fitness center and a trainer, Mother enjoys individual and group exercise on a regular basis. We tease her all the time about having a personal trainer! But it is so beneficial that she can easily take advantage of the treadmill, exercise classes, walking groups, and Tai Chi. Mom Kelley is also involved in an exercise program. Chuck bought his mother her first pair of tennis shoes at the age of 80! She seems to enjoy the activity, and though Papa Kelley is not able to follow directions for his exercise, he does move around during his activity sessions. Exercise and physical activity should be promoted with all seniors.

5. Adequate sleep improves overall functioning. Sleep disturbance is a common complaint of seniors. Some older people sleep too much while others have trouble sleeping. Seek medical assistance to determine if your loved one has a sleep disorder or sleep deprivation. Sometimes medication is indicated, but often sleep can be enhanced if nighttime routines are developed to improve sleep. It is not uncommon for the elderly to sleep much of the day. While occasional naps can be refreshing, deep sleep in the daytime interferes with sustained sleep at night. Again, exercise and activity during the day may decrease sleepiness. Mental stimulation keeps the mind more alert. Lack of stimulation results in more lethargy and sleepiness. More hours spent awake in the daytime may promote more hours of sleep at night.

These helpful hints for dealing with the physical decline of loved ones may seem obvious and simplistic, however, caregivers often become overwhelmed and stressed by the demands of life, forgetting the most obvious strategies.

Parents have previously managed their own lives, but children must gradually get involved. While little can be done to slow the rate of physical decline, much can be done today to promote good health.

Mental Decline

Senior adults also face mental decline. In addition to physical decline, children must help their aging parents face challenges in their mental functioning. Intellectual abilities decrease, including the ability to think clearly and remember accurately. Senior adults often become forgetful and confused. Disorientation may lead to frustration and depression. Mental decline may cause moodiness and withdrawal. For the older adult, the cycle may seem hopeless—aging leads to physical decline, which leads to mental decline, which leads to social decline. Mental decline in parents may be the most difficult symptom of aging for children to understand and manage.

A friend recently discussed the challenges of her mother's six-year decline: "The hardest thing is watching her mind slowly vanish. However, there are even some positives to that. She does not grieve for a friend who dies or a great grandson who was stillborn." She wondered aloud, "Is this God's way of protecting one of His faithful?"

Mental decline of a loved one is difficult to watch. However, even in the loss of a person's mind and memory, there are blessings. Our precious Papa has senile dementia. His mind is confused and his memory is impaired. My husband says that his life is playing like a record album. The needle comes down at different points in his life: Sometimes he is living in his childhood, sometimes he is at work during his career, and other times he is living out news events heard on television. His train of thought is impossible to explain. But we are so grateful that he is content and cared for well. I often think he has just the right amount of dementia—he is enjoying his life, not aware of his limitations.

Cognition is often impaired by the aging process. While several terms are used to describe the symptoms of forgetfulness, confusion, and mental decline, *dementia* is the most common. Dementia is a medical diagnosis for these symptoms, though it is not the name of the disease or diseases that cause the symptoms. Different diseases cause dementia. Therefore, it is important to understand the medical cause as well as how to manage the specific symptoms of dementia.

Adult children who suspect mental decline in their parents should begin to observe their behaviors and discuss their conditions confidentially with family members. The family physician may be helpful in providing objective monitoring of behaviors as well as recommendations for care. While the mental decline associated with dementia is progressive, a person's quality of life can be promoted. Proper evaluation and treatment are essential.

In addition to forgetfulness and confusion, mental decline also results in communication problems, combative behavior, and time disorientation. Aging people have increasing difficulty understanding what is said to them and communicating their own thoughts verbally. Some people have difficulty finding words to express their thoughts. Some talk fluently though their thoughts are rambling and vague. Loved ones must be patient and listen attentively to understand the message. Verbal language problems may increase as the dementia progresses. Comprehension weaknesses may result in uncooperative behavior. Poor understanding of written or spoken language may also be a symptom of dementia. Family members must adjust as their loved one experiences greater communication problems.

These suggestions for improved verbal communication with a person who has a dementing illness are from *The*

36-Hour Day, by Nancy L. Mace and Peter V. Rabins (pp. 38–39):

1. Make sure that your loved one does hear you.
2. Lower the tone or pitch of your voice to better be heard, especially if hearing loss is present.
3. Eliminate distracting noises or activities to focus attention.
4. Use short words and short, simple sentences to help with comprehension.
5. Ask only one simple question at a time.
6. Ask the person to do only one task at a time, not several.
7. Speak slowly, and wait for the person to respond.

When relating to older people, I am grateful for my training as a speech pathologist. Slow, clear speech does seem to help the person with dementia communicate more effectively.

My sweet father-in-law often has difficulty communicating. His conversations tend to ramble and are difficult to follow. My mother-in-law corrects him, identifying his errors and providing the correct information. After 63 years of marriage, it is hard for her to understand his cognitive decline. However, my husband and I have noticed that Papa Kelley responds more positively if we ignore the errors and make general comments in agreement. Family members must learn to adapt to their loved one's decline.

Individuals with dementia may get angry or combative. Sometimes their aggressive behavior is a result of communication disorders and other times it is the result of confusion. Behavior changes are often very upsetting for family members. It is important to remember that it is not a conscious behavior of your loved one. It is the dementia causing the reaction. When your loved one gets agitated, immediately stop what is upsetting and allow time to relax. Do not push them or they may become more agitated. If the uncontrollable behavior continues, medical help may be needed.

When my father-in-law becomes ill with an infection or when he has had surgery, he can become more confused and agitated. The greatest concern is for his safety and the safety of others. Distraction often helps. But his occasional aggressive behavior is very upsetting to everyone since his natural disposition is so pleasant. It is important for family members to remember that it is the illness causing the behavior changes, not the person. Try not to take the agitation personally.

Time becomes irrelevant for those with dementia. There is often an inability to know what time it is or how much time has passed. Since memory is impaired, the person with dementia is unaware of what has transpired in the immediate past. The internal clock may also be affected. People with dementia may be unable to keep a regular schedule for sleeping, waking, and eating. This time confusion can be upsetting to the individual as well as the family. Again, it is not a conscious change in behavior; it is a result of the dementia.

One of the first signs of dementia in my sweet father-in-law was time confusion. He would often wake up at 2:00 A.M. thinking that it was time to get up. He would make the coffee and wake up his wife, not realizing his error. Even though he could read aloud the time on the clock, he did not understand the time of day. Now it is a blessing that Papa has no sense of time. He doesn't know how much time elapses between family visits, so there is no feeling of guilt for children who are unable to visit often. He doesn't know if it has been five minutes, five weeks, or five months since the last visit. He is unaware when his sweetheart is absent, though he loves her daily visits.

One of the most confusing symptoms of dementia is the fluctuation in ability. People with dementia may be able to perform a task appropriately at one time and not at another.

Good days and bad days occur as well as good times of the day and bad. Regular routines and familiar surroundings may help. While fluctuations cannot be explained, they are to be expected if your loved one has dementia. Physical and mental decline are expected as the years pass. It is best to accept the changes while accommodating for the changes in appropriate ways.

It was truly a blessing that our Papa was cognitively able to complete his major business affairs before his dementia progressed. We had become aware that he thought more clearly in the morning, when he was more alert. As the day progressed, he became more confused. In order to adapt to his mental decline, we scheduled meetings with attorneys and realtors in the morning. It is important to recognize cognitive changes in your loved one and make accommodations when possible.

Though space does not allow a full discussion here, it is important to mention Alzheimer's disease, one of the most frequent diagnoses of senior citizens. It is "an irreversible dementia which progresses gradually from forgetfulness to total disability" (*The 36-Hour Day*, page 6). While the cause of this illness is still unknown, autopsies reveal structural changes in the brain. Extensive research is underway, though at the present time there are no known preventions or cures. However, medical interventions have developed which can diminish the behavioral and emotional symptoms of Alzheimer's disease. The Alzheimer's Association provides educational materials and supports scientific research. Many facilities provide specialized programs for patients with Alzheimer's as well as other dementing illnesses.

Social Decline

Social decline typically develops as adults age. As health problems develop and mental acuity diminishes, individuals may withdraw from social interaction, becoming isolated and depressed. Loss of abilities may result in a feeling of sadness or loss of hope. Individuals may become lethargic and listless. A person who has previously been very social and outgoing may become quiet and withdrawn because of neurological changes.

It is so important to keep older people active and as involved with other people as possible. When they become confused, or as their physical health and mental status decline, it may be easier for them to withdraw than adjust to the changes. However, physical and mental activity can stimulate social interaction and improve your loved one's quality of life.

One of the forgotten benefits of alternative living facilities is the emphasis on socialization. Many older adults become isolated when living alone. As their mobility and independence decrease, they see fewer people, get out less often, and their worlds become smaller. Many seniors watch hours of television because it is a passive activity requiring little physical or mental effort. Assisted living centers, skilled nursing homes, and senior day care programs provide for socialization with others as well as physical activity and mental stimulation.

Keep your loved one connected with family members through visits, phone calls, and letters. Take them to church and other group activities for social interaction if possible. Help them stay in touch with special friends and make new friends. Even in their severe decline, parents, especially mothers, are encouraged by time spent with others. Since women are relational human beings, a mother's quality of life is greatly improved by social interaction.

One friend related her precious story of the care of her 94-year-old mother in the advanced stages of Alzheimer's disease. Because her mother had always loved being around people, she visited her regularly and talked to her as if she could understand. Margaret said: "I tell her family news, read Scripture to her, sing to her (she was a church musician for years), and pray with her each day. She is very calm, and often I feel what I tell her or read to her connects. I talk to her as though she can understand everything. I try to be cheerful and positive. I do her nails, style her hair, and *always* put lipstick on her! I try to provide for her needs and give her personal interaction. She may not understand, but I know she enjoys my company."

Chuck and I have seen our parents benefit socially from living in a retirement center. Papa Kelley loves to be around people. He brightens up when someone walks in the room and calls his name. He always has a smile on his face and a joyful greeting. He spends his days sitting in the activity room, surrounded by people who have come to love him and call him friend. Though he may not fully benefit from the interaction of others, Papa loves their company.

Mom Kelley looks forward to lunchtime with "the girls." She enjoys her morning routines—grocery shopping with the group on Monday, exercise on Tuesday, beauty shop on Wednesday, and Bible study on Thursday. She really loves Friday and Saturday mornings in her apartment to read, relax, and watch *Matlock* on TV. She looks forward to Sunday morning at church. Mom Kelley balances her time alone with afternoon dates with her sweetheart, lunch with friends, phone calls from daughters, and visits from family. She has thrived socially since being in a supportive environment. Chuck often says his mother's personality has blossomed and her sense of humor has developed in recent months.

My mother enjoys the companionship of new friends. While at first she was concerned about possible intrusion by close neighbors in an apartment complex, now she benefits from their companionship at meals as well as group outings. The importance of socialization cannot be exaggerated. A daughter can help her mother have more meaning in life if she encourages social interaction in response to social decline.

The daughter of a sweet lady in our church continues to bring her to church on Sundays, though her cognitive abilities are deteriorating. She often makes inappropriate comments or displays unusual behavior, which could be embarrassing to the family. However, she seems to enjoy being with other people and the church members love and accept her. It is important for Christians to minister to those who are aging and to be understanding about the needs of the family members.

While the decline of parents is a difficult progression to observe, it is essential for adult children to recognize the decline and respond appropriately. No one benefits when decline is denied. Instead, make the most of every moment and adjust together through difficult stages. Your love, support, and companionship will mean so much to your mother as she experiences physical, mental, and social decline.

Mother-Daughter Reflections

1. When did you begin to notice decline in your mother's overall condition? What were her first signs of decline?

2. List some physical challenges your mother faces.

3. Do you notice any areas of mental decline in your mother?

4. Evaluate your mother's social strengths and areas that need support.

5. In what ways are you and your mother trying to prepare for, or compensate for, declines in physical, mental, or social ability?

Chapter Four

Making Hard Decisions

L ife is filled with decisions. In fact, decisions are required every moment of one's life. Some decisions are conscious, requiring consideration and thought, while others are unconscious or automatic, resulting from reaction or response. Some decisions are major and life changing, while other decisions are minor and have little consequence. As a person ages, difficult decisions seem more frequent. Adult daughters and their aging mothers must learn how to make these hard decisions together.

Ideally, it is best for parents and children to discuss serious issues before decisions are needed. A crisis does not allow time for thoughtful decision making. Advanced directives help families make hard decisions. Talking with your parents about the future may be just as uncomfortable as that teenage talk about "the birds and the bees," but both are important. If you have not had "the future talk" with your parents, find an appropriate time to talk openly and honestly. Both you and your parents will later be grateful for the clear understanding of personal wishes.

Vonda Skinner Skelton summarized the tough questions to ask your parents in her article "Can We Talk?" (*Christian Single*, May 2005). She divided the questions into three categories and listed them one by one. The list may be a helpful outline for the discussion you have with your parents.

Health Care Issues

1. If you are terminally ill with no chance of recovery, do you want feeding tubes or life support?
2. Do you want to be an organ donor?
3. Where do you want to live if you are unable to care for yourself?

Legal Advice

1. Do you have an up-to-date will?
2. Who has agreed to be your executor?
3. If incapacitated, who do you want to handle your medical and legal decisions?
4. Where are your important papers, insurance policies, will, and safe deposit key?
5. Do you have long-term care insurance?

Last Wishes

1. Do you prefer burial or cremation?
2. Who would you like to speak and what songs do you want played at your funeral?

3. Do you have a special message you would like the speaker to share?

It would be helpful to have this discussion as a family so parents and children can be informed. If you or your parents are uncomfortable or unable to have a face-to-face conversation, ask them to respond to these questions in writing. Written records are preferable anyway, especially concerning legal issues. Some people even tape record or videotape these discussions as a permanent record for the future.

My assistant, Christian, recently took a class at the seminary on death and loss. As an assignment, she developed her funeral plans and discussed them with her family. Christian said it seemed strange to be planning her own funeral, and it was even more difficult to discuss the topic with her parents. While her last wishes may change as her life continues, the discussion was a valuable experience for her and her parents. Undoubtedly, it will be easier now for her to talk with her parents about their last wishes. In fact, Christian reports that her parents have initiated the discussion of their wishes on several occasions.

Our friend Becky recently attempted to discuss the future with her parents. She was hoping they would be open to moving in with her some time in the near future. However, her father adamantly responded, "I have a home." His answer let her know in no uncertain terms that he wasn't ready for the move yet. However, Becky has now had the talk with her parents, who may be more open to discussion in the future.

I am grateful that I have had the talk with each of my parents. We continue to dialogue about the future as time passes. It was very natural for the Kelleys to make final arrangements since he was a funeral director for more than 40 years. My own mother handled these medical and legal issues years ago and has her business affairs in order. It is such a blessing to know their personal wishes, though difficult decisions are still inevitable.

The future is certainly a serious topic of discussion. However, it may help to relieve the pressure with some humor. My dad laughs as my sister and I tease him about who will be "stuck with him when he is old." We jokingly pass him off to the other like a football. Then we finally agree to take care of him. Now we tell his wife Becky how grateful we are that she will be his caregiver. Often my dad initiates the joke. But we all know that either my sister or I would do anything in the world to care for our dad. Humor can often be helpful when discussing serious issues or facing hard decisions.

Though the Kelleys had considered many future plans, we were still faced with hard decisions when Papa became ill in the summer of 2002. It was quite a shock to Mom Kelley when the doctor said he could no longer live independently at home. Our family joined together to help her make some serious decisions.

A friend who is a social worker providing elder care in the city of New Orleans recommended a helpful resource to us. The book, *The 36-Hour Day: A Family Guide to Caring for Persons with Alzheimer Disease, Related Dementing Illnesses, and Memory Loss in Later Life*, by Nancy Mace and Peter Rabins, has been extremely beneficial to us. Chuck and I immediately bought a copy and read it from cover to cover. We purchased copies for Mom Kelley and each of his four sisters. We were grateful for the professional advice at our time of need. Our greatest strength came from the Lord, who led us and provided for us each step of the way. For the Christian, faith in the Lord is the greatest source of strength.

In this chapter, several types of decisions will be considered. While personal circumstances may vary, most families will face these inevitable challenges. Daughters will find themselves helping their mothers with choices concerning living arrangements, medical care, and financial management.

Living Arrangements

Most people desire to continue living independently, to provide completely for themselves. However, the time comes for many older people to receive assistance. Children often become concerned about an aging parent's ability to care for personal needs and maintain safety. Subtle signs may be overlooked, but eventually changes cannot be ignored. The individual may be unaware of her own decline or may deny her weaknesses.

Significant decline forces decisions that are life changing. However, parents may resist giving up their means of independence. If they are professionals, they may no longer be able to perform their work. Their employers may suggest retirement or disability. The time to give up a job varies based on the type of work and the complexity of skills. As time passes, parents may no longer drive safely. Decreased vision, coordination, and cognition will determine when driving should cease. Giving up car keys is one of the most difficult life changes and a major loss of independence.

Another common marker of decline is a person's inability to manage money. Simple tasks such as making change, paying bills, or balancing a checkbook may become difficult. Parents who have managed their money proficiently in the past may make unwise investments or spend money foolishly. Unfortunately, financial scams are frequent with seniors who may naively accept a phone solicitor's offer. Concerned children must become increasingly involved in helping their parents with daily living skills such as money management.

Independent living. Most people would choose to live alone as long as possible. For many healthy seniors, independent living is a realistic option. They may continue to live in their family homes or apartments with minimal assistance from others. Children may begin greater involvement in their parents' lives, though mostly in a supportive role.

If your mother is still living independently, be sure to stay in frequent contact with her through telephone calls and visits. It is important to notice changes as soon as possible. Offer to assist with more difficult tasks, accompany her to medical appointments, and consult about financial matters. Talk openly about her increasing needs and your desire to help.

I recently heard a term that describes the individual who coordinates the care of another person. The term "care agent" seems an appropriate label for many daughters caring for their mothers. In the same way that an insurance agent or real estate agent assists a client in receiving services, a family member or friend may serve as a "care agent" for aging parents. I consider this my present role with our parents. While I do not actually provide for their physical care, I am responsible for coordinating their services and making sure their needs are being met. With the help of a care agent, many senior adults may remain independent for years longer. Professional care agents can also be hired by families who need outside support.

The decision about alternative living arrangements may be the most difficult parent-child decision. When possible, a gradual transition from independent to dependent living is best. The tremendous development of continued care or life-care facilities in America often makes it possible for an individual to move from independent to assisted to dependent living all within the same facility. The "one big move" certainly reduces some stress and provides for their needs more appropriately. It is often more economic financially as well.

Some parents refuse to leave their homes, or their children choose to provide in-home care. Family members, friends, and neighbors are usually the first to help. Home services can be provided through sitters, aides, or nurses. Assistance can be offered for medical care, safety, personal hygiene, nutrition, and recreation. Many products are available to adapt the home for older people. Adult day care programs offer several hours of structured recreation and social recreation. Meals can be provided through local programs. However, as more support is needed, the individual may progress from independent living to assisted living arrangements.

Assisted living. Many facilities market specialized care for seniors in a more homelike setting with supervised care. While the individual may live alone in a room or apartment, limited medical services are also provided. Assistance with daily living and medication management, as well as social activities and emergency intervention are offered. Assisted living arrangements are available in separate facilities or as a part of life-care centers. These facilities are often a step between living independently and living in a nursing home.

Chuck and I learned an important lesson about living arrangements as we visited facilities with his mother. While Papa needed 24-hour nursing care, Mom Kelley was still independent. Of course, her heart's desire was to live with her husband. We began looking for assisted living for both of them. Over and over again we were told by professionals that "the healthy spouse lives down to the level of the unhealthy spouse." The three of us finally understood that assisted living was not the best setting for Papa or Mom. He would not receive the level of care he needed and she would be stressed by the responsibility of his care. What an answer to prayer it was when Mom concluded that Papa needed the best care! A life-care facility was perfect for them. He lives dependently in skilled nursing, and she lives independently, while both are under the same roof. Chuck loves to remind his mother, "You are only an elevator ride away from your sweetheart."

Decisions about living arrangements are difficult and must be made carefully with consideration for individual needs.

Dependent living. Many seniors with increasing medical needs and decreasing cognitive ability become totally dependent on others. Nursing homes or skilled nursing facilities may be needed on a short-term basis after serious illness or surgery or on a long-term basis for progressive problems. They provide 24-hour nursing care as well as housing and all meals. A wide range of amenities and services exist among nursing homes. Financial means, medical needs, and geographical location often determine the choice of facilities.

The term "nursing home" produces a negative image for many people. Initially, thoughts of depressing, crowded, unsanitary places come to mind. Past experiences or movie stereotypes may be responsible for those false impressions. Those concerns are rarely true today. There is a greater demand for skilled nursing facilities since people are living longer. Governmental regulations also protect patients and promote better care. Often, nursing homes are the best alternative for an ill or disabled person. Be open as you consider living arrangements and seek to meet your loved one's needs in the most appropriate setting.

A dear friend named Bet agreed with her family that her 97-year-old mother would be best cared for in a nursing home. Though it was a tough decision, they knew she would benefit from the medical services and the social interaction. Bet reported:

> After Mother broke her hip at age 97, we tried to have 24-hour care for her in her home. But those hired were unskilled. She and Daddy made it clear to us through the years that they would never live with any of us. So when she became dependent, it seemed clear that a nursing home was the best option.

Since Mother is gregarious, we knew that she would enjoy the other residents of the home. She needs and enjoys community. Since her sister was already in the same home and it was just a few miles from us, we know now that it was the right decision.

Though decisions about your loved one's future are difficult, it is essential for caregivers to make the best decision—even when it hurts.

Medical Care

Decisions about medical care are some of the most difficult challenges facing seniors. Children must become more involved as the years pass and health problems develop. They must respect their parent's desires, seek professional help, offer wise advice, and provide needed support to their parents. Some parents contract serious illnesses or develop significant disabilities that require specialized care. Even healthy senior adults find themselves taking more medicine, seeing more doctors, and feeling more aches and pains. Minor illnesses may become major as the body weakens and the healing process slows down. The involvement of adult children becomes necessary.

Senior adults may be unaccustomed to doctors and resist medical intervention. They may also become overwhelmed by the different specialties and number of doctors. Caring children can help them find the appropriate physician and adjust to the need for medical care. It is important for the parent and the child to have confidence in the doctor. Since a daughter will often provide transportation and physical care, she should be involved in the parent's choice of a physician. This decision may prove difficult and may lead them to several doctors. Try to be patient and persevere until both are satisfied with the doctor.

Many illnesses will require specialized treatments. One of the first difficult decisions may be whether or not to pursue treatment at all. Such a serious decision should have the support of the entire family. Decisions about medications are often difficult. Some medicines that treat the illness have negative side effects. Many medicines are very expensive and stress a senior adult's fixed income. Other medications may be controversial or unproven. Families need to agree about medications. It is important that all the parent's physicians know all medications being taken. The intake of medicines must often be monitored. Assisted living and skilled nursing facilities insure that medicines are taken at the right time and in the right dosages.

Decisions about surgery may also be difficult. Some surgeries are lifesaving while others may simply be life enhancing. Upon the doctor's recommendation and after thorough discussion, families are better prepared to make surgical decisions with their loved ones. Caregivers should keep in mind that recovery from surgery is typically slower for older adults, especially those who are ill.

In 1999, Papa Kelley was diagnosed with cancer. A malignant growth above his eye had spread and resulted in the removal of his right eye and some surrounding area. His surgery disfigured his face significantly. He was able to make his own decision to forego reconstructive plastic surgery. While additional surgery would have improved his appearance, it would have also been risky due to his increased health problems. Our family and his physicians were supportive of his decision. It helped tremendously that he accepted his altered appearance with joy and peace. We are grateful that he has enjoyed years of life since his cancer developed. Surgery decisions are often difficult and may need family intervention.

The need for hospitalization may pose a challenge to parents and their children. As health declines and medical crises occur, hospitalization may be required more often. It can be a trying time for the patient and family. Your parent will benefit from the presence of someone she knows while she is hospitalized. A family member or friend can provide companionship as well as assistance. Older adults with cognitive impairment may become confused in the unfamiliar environment of a hospital and agitated from pain or discomfort. Because hospitalization is inevitably traumatic, some people prefer not to be hospitalized. Again, there is no perfect solution to the challenging problem. Agreement between the parent and children is important.

Another hard medical decision for seniors is duration of treatment. Terminal illnesses and progressive diseases may require aggressive treatment. The time may come for the family to decide whether to continue or discontinue treatment. Each circumstance is unique, and each decision is based on the family's particular background, experiences, and beliefs. The most important considerations are the comfort and dignity of your loved one. It is preferred that the treatment decisions be made by the patient. Living wills and other legal papers document the medical wishes of an individual. However, families must often make treatment decisions in consultation with doctors and in consensus with one another. Ultimately, the duration of your loved one's life is in God's hands. You can be at peace knowing that God is caring for the one you love.

Financial Management

Seeking assistance with finances and discussing confidential money matters is difficult for most people, especially seniors who have frugally managed their money for years. As your parents become less mentally astute and their financial matters become more complicated, you may need to become more actively involved. The assistance of a financial advisor and certified public accountant (CPA) may be helpful in managing investments and handling taxes. Legal advice is also essential before your parents become unable to handle their own business affairs.

While this section cannot include a thorough discussion, some factors concerning financial and legal issues will be mentioned. Initial assessment of your parent's sources of income and expenses is necessary. A retired person typically lives on a fixed income and faces the impact of inflation on cost of living. Current expenses as well as potential costs for care must be considered in light of rising prices and increasing infirmity. Identify your loved one's total assets and financial resources such as pensions, Social Security income, retirement or disability benefits, savings accounts, real estate investments, automobiles, and other sources of income. Locate policies for life insurance, health insurance, and long-term care as well as other automobile or home owners' documents. Pursue tax breaks available to older Americans and for medical deductions. Investigate state, federal, and private resources for financial assistance. Secure Medicare and possibly Medicaid benefits. It is also imperative for a responsible party to be added to the checking and savings accounts for release of information and withdrawals.

A major decision is the senior adult's appointment of a power of attorney. Though it may be emotionally difficult to relinquish financial control, it is essential for business and legal action. Legal arrangements must be made while a person is mentally competent or capable of making important decisions. Most states have "durable power of attorney," which authorizes someone to act in behalf of the person after she becomes unable to make her own decisions. Some states have separate documents for business and medical power of attorney, while other states have a single document. Legal counsel is essential to protect your loved one and provide for financial assistance.

God truly intervened in our family, prompting Chuck's parents to finalize their wills and power of attorney before Papa became unable to handle their financial affairs. Within a year, those documents were registered and Papa was able to sign final contracts on the sales of their home and other properties. Though Mom Kelley and Chuck now serve as Papa's power of attorney, it is a blessing that he could complete those important transactions. Now everything is in place for future decisions to be made for him that are in his best interest.

In recent years, I have been called upon by our parents to become involved in their financial affairs. The complicated world of business and finance is definitely beyond my field of expertise. However, at my parents' requests, I have begun sitting in on their meetings with the financial advisor and discussing their money matters with them. I have certainly learned about stocks and bonds, savings and money market accounts, diversified investments, and tax credits. My role is supportive now but may become more directive in the future. I try to listen carefully and take notes about investment returns so that I can clarify the details for my "moms." As they consider financial decisions, I encourage their wise choices and offer advice when requested. I reassure them when they become anxious about the limitations of fixed incomes. Managing their money and balancing their budgets seem to be a growing responsibility. Together we can handle the challenge of financial matters.

Major decisions are always difficult. Those decisions concerning your parents may be particularly challenging. Decisions must be approached with careful consideration and persistent prayer. Christians should be sensitive to God's leadership as we help our parents make hard decisions or we make them on our parents' behalf. While a crisis will sometimes force a decision, at other times God will prompt the heart of His children to take proactive measures.

Ideally, parents will make many money decisions for themselves. Often decisions will be made collectively as a family. Sometimes designated adult children must make decisions for their parents. While parents may be primarily concerned about maintaining independence, children may objectively see the realistic needs of their parents. Of primary importance is confidence in the Lord to provide for all needs and give guidance in making difficult decisions.

Mother-Daughter Reflections

1. What are some hard decisions you and your parents have had to make? How has the decision process affected your relationship?

2. Have you talked with your mother about living arrangements? What are her present needs and her future wishes?

3. What options for medical care have you discussed with your mother? Do you know her decisions about physicians, desire for treatment, and duration of treatment?

4. Have you and your mother discussed her financial affairs? What legal and business arrangements have been made?

5. What resources help you and your mother make difficult decisions? How does your faith affect your decisions?

Chapter Five

Building a New Relationship

Relationships with other people may bring great joy to life, but those same relationships can also produce tremendous strain and pain. All relationships require work as the people and circumstances change over time. Some personalities complicate relationships from the beginning. People can choose to develop friendships or distance themselves from neighbors and colleagues who are not agreeable, but family members should learn to get along with each other since their relationship is ongoing. Healthy relationships among relatives take effort and cooperation. The work is worth it as the relationships deepens.

The unique relationship between mother and daughter changes over time. As the years pass and circumstances change, mother and daughter often move from a parent-child relationship of definite authority and submission to a peer relationship of friend-friend and later a reversed relationship of child-parent. In each phase of the relationship, love and respect can promote a healthy transition.

Opinions differ about actual role reversals as parents age and adult children become the caregivers. Some believe that children never actually "parent their parents," while others conclude that care of aging parents is much like raising children. Certainly parents always deserve the respect and honor of their children. However, in practical ways, the care needed by parents changes the relationship. As always, change does not have to be bad. Adult children can see many blessings and benefits of their role reversals. Raising parents should not be a chore or a demeaning task, but a precious privilege and a natural progression in life.

When the idea for this book developed in my mind and heart, the title *Raising Moms* was obvious to me. I had often referred to the support I give my mothers as "raising my moms." Many of my peers were in similar situations of caring for their own families while meeting the increasing needs of their parents. They agreed that in many ways the care of their aging parents was much like the care of their younger children.

A social worker friend warned me about the harshness of the title of my book. Her concern was valid. Parents will always be parents and should never be treated like children. They should always be respected, even when they are unable to care for their own needs. While I certainly agree with her opinion, I also believe that parenting is a high calling. The "parenting of parents" is a great blessing, as is the raising of children. The understanding that the time comes when a daughter raises her mother does not imply disrespect but recognizes that the roles have changed. The daughter now relates to her mother more like she relates to her own children as her mother's need for care increases. Daughters can care for their mothers in their later years and maintain respect for them as parents. In fact, I personally believe that a daughter's respect for her mother is demonstrated tangibly as she tenderly cares for her.

In this chapter, attention will be given to the changing and maturing relationship between mother and daughter. The early relationship is influenced by the mother's responsibility to the child. As the child reaches adulthood, that relationship often develops into a friendship, a bond between peers. In later years, the child must often assume responsibility for the parent, in many ways reversing the roles in the relationship while maintaining feelings of love and respect.

Parent-Child

In the beginning, when God created man and woman, He gave them the command, "be fruitful and multiply" (Genesis 1:28 NKJV). His plan not only brought about the procreation of life, but provided for meaningful relationships within families. At the time of their children's birth, Christian parents are reminded of the awesome creative power of God when they see their newborn babies. The Bible clearly teaches parents the responsibility of raising their children. It contains clear principles for bringing them up in the nurture and admonition of the Lord.

Parents are to love and care for their children not just in the early years but throughout life. Parents are to provide not only for the physical and mental needs of their children, but their emotional and spiritual needs as well. When children are very young, parents focus on ensuring that their basic needs for food, clothing, and shelter are being met. As the children grow, parents begin stimulating them developmentally and teaching them right from wrong. While schools provide education and churches offer inspiration, parents are the primary teachers for their children. The parent-child relationship is described by **teaching.**

Christian parents have the added responsibility of teaching their children spiritual truths so they can live godly lives. The Old Testament instructs parents to teach the principles of God's Word diligently to their children: "Talk about them when you sit in your house and when you walk along the road, when you lie down and when you get up" (Deuteronomy 6:7). Parents are to follow the law of God personally and speak His truths from generation to generation (Psalm 78:1–4). The New Testament affirms the responsibility of parents to teach their children the way of the Lord. Like Lois and Eunice, grandmothers and mothers are to pass along a legacy of faith to the next generation (2 Timothy 1:3–5). Paul summed up the biblical mandate, speaking to fathers in Ephesians 6:4: "Bring them [your children] up in the training and instruction of the Lord."

Parents must lead their children in God's way through loving and consistent discipline. While the world presents many child-rearing methods, often weakening the role of parents in a child's life, the Bible is clear. Parents are to "train up a child in the way he should go, and when he is old he will not depart from it" (Proverbs 22:6 NKJV). The promise is given by God to parents who teach their children His ways so that they will have a strong spiritual foundation for life. While some children choose the path of foolishness, others will return to the faith of their parents. Discipline of children is not merely administering punishment, but is mostly nurturing development of godly virtues.

One of a Christian parent's most precious privileges is leading her child to a personal relationship with the Lord. A parent's lessons in faith by word and example plant seeds of faith in the child's heart. At the age of accountability and through the prompting of the Holy Spirit, a child is led to trust Jesus as Savior. Parents are blessed by the investment of their spiritual training when children profess a personal acceptance of Jesus.

Training and discipline are essential dynamics of the parent-child relationship. While children may not appreciate the efforts of their parents at the time, as they mature, most children acknowledge the profound impact of parents on their lives. Often children regret their misbehavior and repent of rebellion. The unconditional love of parents nurtures the relationship through rocky roads. Daughters often confess their faults in an effort to strengthen their relationships with their mothers. However, guilt is a natural response of most women. God can help daughters overcome their feelings of guilt.

My sister and I often laugh about not being the perfect people our mother wants us to be. Of course, Mother doesn't expect us to be perfect. Yet she doesn't seem aware of the guilt she imposes on us by commenting on our appearance, housekeeping, or cooking. She sincerely means well. However, as the children she has raised, we hear in her comments disappointment for not learning from her training. Daughters tend to assume guilt from well-meaning mothers. That guilt can strain the mother-daughter relationship.

Cathy Guisewite said it like this in her cartoon strip *Cathy*: "Mother, food, love, career: the four major guilt groups." I saw a T-shirt at the mall that captured these feelings perfectly: "My mother is the travel agent of guilt trips." Guilt is a common feeling among daughters who want to please their mothers. These feelings of guilt impact the parent-child relationship and must be dealt with before mother and daughter can become friends.

As the years quickly pass, the young child becomes an adult and the parenting role changes. Major milestones in a child's life, such as entering first grade, beginning to drive, going on the first date, and going away to college, are profound reminders to a mother that her child is growing up. My sister, Mitzi, is sending a son away to college this year. She is trying so hard to be excited for his opportunity, though she is sad he will be leaving home. She keeps telling herself, "Our relationship will never again be the same—he's grown up." And, while that is true, she can work to develop a new and even deeper relationship with her grown son.

Mitzi has been remembering the trip she took with my mother to take me to my college, which was out of state. While Mother was thrilled for her elder daughter to attend Baylor University, she dreaded the separation. Mitzi jokingly recalls the ten-hour drive from Waco, Texas, back to New Orleans with Mother crying all the way. Mother was faced with the reality that I was growing up.

The passage from childhood to adulthood is a natural part of the cycle of life. Mother and daughter must navigate the changes and develop a new relationship. Open communication and frequent visits help the parent-child duo become friends. The friend-friend stage can actually encompass more years than the parenting or caregiving stages. With love, acceptance, and understanding, mother and daughter can become good friends.

Friend-Friend

While the parent-child bond continues throughout life, the relationship often develops into a friendship as the two adults share life experiences. If the parent-child stage is characterized by teaching, then the friend-friend stage can be characterized by **sharing.** Mother and daughter are both adults and have many similarities. Daughters often report close friendships with their mothers during their adult years.

Making friends with your mother is a way of acknowledging that you have grown up. When you take a job, marry, or have a child, you can suddenly relate to your mother. You often seek her advice and support. You become a friend while enjoying the pride of your parents. Mothers by nature are loyal to their children and always boast about their accomplishments, sometimes in excess. An adult daughter is strengthened by a relationship with her mother that adds friendship to nurturing. Most daughters desire independence from their mothers, though at times, only a mother can soothe the pains.

Even more so than good friends, mothers know their daughters like a book, love them unconditionally, and desire their companionship at all times. During adulthood, daughters can develop special friendships with their mothers. Often, tensions in the relationship must be resolved. Sometimes mothers have difficulty accepting their daughters as adults. If issues exist about dependence and control, mothers and daughters may have trouble being friends. Time and energy must be exerted by both to work out these differences and develop a meaningful friendship. If the differences are extreme, professional help may encourage mothers and daughters to restore communication and rebuild trust. The mother-daughter relationship is worth the effort and expense.

I have enjoyed building a new relationship with my mother. While we are not exactly alike, we share many common values and interests. We love spending time together and have learned to negotiate our differences through give and take. We recently enjoyed a trip together. The two of us took a three-night cruise on a Mississippi River boat. We had a wonderful time talking, sightseeing, and eating. There were moments of impasse when we had to decide what to do or where to go. Because of our love for each other, we were willing to put aside our own desires and compromise. I am grateful when Mother describes me as a best friend or says she can talk with me about anything. It is precious to share life with my mother, who is also my friend. Our friendship also makes it easier for me to assist her with her increasing needs.

Child-Parent

The transition from parenting to friendship may be more clearly marked by milestones. The transition for mothers and daughters from friendship to caregiving may be more gradual. Sometimes a sudden illness or traumatic event will force the sudden change of roles. Usually, the relationship progresses naturally over time. As parents become less able to care for themselves, daughters often step in to help. The parenting stage is characterized by teaching, the friendship stage is characterized by sharing, and the final child-parent stage of the mother-daughter relationship is characterized by **caring.** Daughters often become the caretakers of their parents.

My friend Chris has recently moved into the child-parent relationship with her mother. For Chris, this transition has been bittersweet. She finds herself missing someone mothering her. "Instead of going to my mother for advice, she is coming to me. It's not a bad thing at all, but there are times I would love to have a mother nurturing me." This feeling is true for most daughters, but we must accept that time changes the roles we play with our mothers.

Recent *USA Today* reports gave interesting statistics about the numbers of women caring for others:

- 61% of caregivers are female
- the average caregiver age is 46 years old
- the average age of care recipients is 77 years old
- 66% of caregivers have some college experience
- 79% of caregivers spend 20 hours a week or more providing for someone 50 years or older
- 66% of caregivers are married
- 41% of caregivers have children under 18 living at home
- 52% of caregivers are employed full-time

In another article, research demonstrated that more adults today than ever before are providing care for their aging parents. However, the increase in caregiving has just begun.

- 23% of all Americans are caring for a relative or friend 50 or older
- caregivers spend an average of $221 per month on the care recipients' expenses
- the median family income of a caregiver household is $35,000

Elder care will become even more common in 2011 when 77 million baby boomers turn 65. The US Census Bureau predicts that by 2050 the 65-and-over population will grow from 12% to 21% of the total population (*USA Today* February 17, 2004, and April 6, 2004). Parenting of parents is becoming an increasing reality every year. Because there are more women than men in the general population and women as a whole live longer than men, daughters or daughters-in-law will most often be caring for their mothers.

Caring for an aging parent will be challenging physically and emotionally. Mothers and daughters will vary in their responses to this relationship change. Patience, communication, and understanding are needed by both parties to make a smooth transition into the caregiving stage. Information and support are available to assist in decisions. The church can also be supportive of senior adults and their caregiving children. A team effort is essential in healthy management of this caring stage.

It may be helpful to recognize the typical ways that older people adapt to caregiving. In his book *Loving Your Parents When They Can No Longer Love You*, Terry Hargrave suggests four basic methods of adaptation by seniors (pages 95–101):

1. The "Make Lemonade" Type—Some older adults accept the limitations that life brings and respond positively, as in the old adage: "If life hands you lemons, make lemonade." These parents will usually be cooperative with caregiving and make the work as pleasant as possible.

2. The "Pretend It's Not Happening" Type—Some older people deny life changes and try to make their lives work without recognizing decline. They will often resist help and get angry at interference. Defensive reactions must be countered with persistence and patience.

3. The "Poor Pitiful Me" Type—Some older adults, unlike the "Pretend It's Not Happening" type, thrive on the attention of others and seek complete caregiving. They often become helpless and totally dependent on others. They feel sorry for themselves and want the sympathy of others. While some care is truly needed, these older adults must be encouraged to do what they can for themselves. Limits must be set and only necessary caregiving should be provided.

4. The "Whatever" Type—Other senior adults respond passively to the process of aging. They may feel helpless to face the challenges. Depression may develop. It may be helpful to reflect back with them on the blessings of life. These parents generally accept caregiving with little problem, though they need extra emotional support.

Adult children must seek to understand their parents' responses to aging as they also identify their own reactions. It is difficult for children to see their parents decline. The relationship inevitably changes as the aging parents weaken and need care from others. It will help everyone involved to work together at developing a new, healthy relationship.

Of course, it has been difficult for Mom Kelley to observe the decline in her husband of 64 years. Chuck and I seek to reassure her as she reports decreases in his physical or mental status. Chuck lovingly suggests to his mother that his changed behavior or increased need for assistance is Papa's "new norm." It seems to help her understand that the gradual changes are progressive and his condition is irreversible. She becomes less emotional talking about his problems and focuses more on his positive attributes. We are grateful that our parents have responded to their life changes positively and have been grateful for our caregiving.

Mothers and daughters learn a powerful life lesson when they make a gradual transition in their relationship over time. Sweet memories of the early parent-child relationship as well as special moments shared as friend to friend better prepare mother and daughter for the role reversal in later years. While challenges are inevitable, a strong bond can strengthen both mother and daughter. The parent-child relationship of twilight years can be the best time of life. God can lead and guide as He blesses a mother and daughter who love and care for each other in each stage of their relationship.

Mother-Daughter Reflections

1. What is your opinion about adult children "parenting their parents"? Can you continue to demonstrate respect for your parents while beginning to provide for their care?

2. How do you remember your childhood? Describe some positive and negative memories of the parent-child relationship?

3. Do you consider your mother your friend? What issues did the two of you resolve to develop a friendship?

4. Describe yourself as a caregiver. What are your responsibilities in life in addition to raising your mother? How do you handle your many responsibilities?

5. What type of response has your mother had to the aging process? Refer back to the adaptation methods suggested by Terry Hargrave and describe her general response.

Chapter Six

Maintaining Communication

Communication is one of the most unique and challenging dynamics of human relationships. While it is simply the exchange of ideas and information with words, gestures, or writing, communication is complicated by the nature of its interactive process. The accurate transmission of a message involves a speaker who can capture thoughts into words and a listener who can perceive the correct meaning. People spend their lifetime trying to understand what other people are saying. Relationships can be strengthened or weakened by effective or ineffective communication.

The process of communication often diminishes as an individual ages, especially with cognitive decline or neurological impairment. Loved ones must work even harder to stay in touch with each other as the years pass. Children must invest time in talking regularly with their parents. Daughters must listen lovingly to the expressed and unexpressed needs of their mothers.

Speech is powerful. The spoken word can either encourage or discourage, help or hurt. The Bible teaches Christians to control the tongue and speak only words of kindness. James 3:1–12 teaches that the tongue is so powerful, it is like a fire that must be tamed. It is true that words can bless or curse. Christians must seek strength from the Lord to control their tongues when speaking to their older parents and other people. They must follow the wise counsel of Paul in Ephesians 4:29: "No rotten talk should come from your mouth, but only what is good for the building up of someone in need, in order to give grace to those who hear."

Communication involves more than talking; it requires listening. Most people talk more freely than they listen. The Book of Proverbs teaches the importance of listening with understanding to those who speak:

1. "A man with understanding keeps silent" (Proverbs 11:12).
2. "A fool does not delight in understanding, but only wants to show off his opinions" (Proverbs 18:2).
3. "The one who gives an answer before he listens—this is foolishness and disgrace for him" (Proverbs 18:13).
4. "Do you see a man who speaks too soon? There is more hope for a fool than for him" (Proverbs 29:20).

If only the wise sage was instructing men and not women to listen and understand. It is clear, however, that these biblical truths apply to all mankind. In fact, women who like to talk need to adhere carefully to these teachings from God to listen with understanding.

Listening is half of the two-way dialogue of communication. Words must be clearly spoken and accurately heard. Verbal language is not the only means of communication in human relationships. People use nonverbal communication as well as verbal. In fact, less than one third of a message is communicated through words; the majority of meaning is expressed nonverbally. Body language, facial expressions, gestures, and tone of voice are also means of communication. Feelings as well as facts are exchanged through verbal and nonverbal communication, as well as written language. Adults often write words to express their thoughts to others, who read the words to gain understanding.

Continued Conversation

Throughout the relationship, a parent and child seek to communicate with each other. At different developmental stages, communication between them is more difficult than at other times. Adolescence probably challenges communication between parent and child more than any other stage. However, parents and children who love each other must continually work at communicating clearly with each other. Parents typically take the initiative in communication in the early years. Later in life, children may become the initiators as their aging parents become less fluent. Daughters caring for their mothers must invest the time and energy needed for effective communication.

Our friend Debbie has a sweet relationship with her mother, who lives near her. Ongoing communication has encouraged their closeness. Debbie and her mother talk often, at least once a week, and many times even more often. They also enjoy regular "girls nights out," dinner and a movie. Debbie shared that her mother is "the first person I call when I need prayer for a concern, and she calls me for the same." Active communication has been a key to their healthy relationship.

With all people, but especially with older adults, communication must be consistent and regular. Conversations should take place regularly and with frequency. Busy daughters need to talk with their mothers often. Older mothers who have more available time want to hear from their daughters. To ensure regular interaction with my mother and Chuck's mother, I have set a minimum standard for my communication with them. I try to talk with my moms every day and see them every week. While our travel schedules and ministry commitments do not always guarantee my regular communication, I work toward those goals. If we have more interaction than the minimum, that's a "grace gift." I also have discovered that my moms hesitate to call me since they know our busy schedules. So, I must initiate communication without failure.

Communication with aging parents must also be concise and repetitive. Information should be shared simply and clearly to ensure the accurate meaning. The message should be repeated several times and in several ways. Communication challenges often arise when the speaker assumes the listener understands the meaning of the message. The more important a message, the more essential it is to clarify and reinforce it. Comprehension and memory fade with aging, so special considerations are required. But it never hurts for the messenger to work on clarity. Mother and daughter both benefit from repetition and conciseness.

My mother recently accompanied Chuck and me on a trip. While we verbally reviewed the schedule, Mother asked me to write down the times. She admitted that she is prone to confuse details and forget specifics more often now. I am grateful that she has willingly acknowledged a change in her abilities and mentioned it to me. I always type up a schedule for Mom

Kelley when family members visit. The itinerary keeps all of us on schedule, and it gives her activities to anticipate.

Above all, communication between mother and daughter should be caring and compassionate. Love and concern is expressed in both words and actions. Time must be taken and consideration must be given to the feelings and emotions of the other person. Tone of voice and facial expression must consistently reflect the kindness of words. Mother and daughter may develop a language of their own—a loving message may be exchanged often without words. Deep, meaningful communication at the emotional level does take practice.

In her book *Forty Days of Care for the Caregiver*, Vicki Gilliam suggests ways to use words constructively when giving care. Conversations between mother and daughter need to accentuate the positive and avoid the negative. The content of conversation can greatly impact a mother's condition and the family relationship, so be careful to maintain positivity in your caregiving conversations.

Negative: Harsh or angry words, criticism, or judgmental statements should be avoided. Impulsive, impatient responses should be controlled. Think and pray before speaking so your words will not hurt or discourage.

Positive: Laugh, sing, and pray together. Read the same Scripture passages and books so you can discuss them or read to your loved one to promote conversation. Use words to build up and strengthen. Reflect back on past accomplishments or precious memories.

Conversation with our Papa has become more challenging as his dementia progresses. He does not clearly understand the meaning of our words and he often cannot express himself coherently. He can read words in the newspaper, on the television, or on signs, but does not know what they mean. He does talk a lot. His initial comments are typically his automatic pleasantries or familiar sayings:

"How's my Rhonda?"

"It's been a great day."

"So good to see you."

"There's my friend."

"I knew you would come."

However, the more he talks, the more confused Papa gets. Though it takes some effort, it is important that we keep talking to him and that we keep him talking.

I have developed several conversational routines for my visits with Papa. I talk about the day of the week and the activities of the day to orient him. I talk through the list of his children and grandchildren so he can stay connected with family. He seems to enjoy the conversation, and I know that I do.

Chuck and I have marveled over Papa's great recall of Scripture and hymns. Even when he cannot carry on a conversation, he can quote a verse or recite some words to a song. We often start a familiar Scripture, which he will then complete, or sing a favorite song so he can join in with us. When Papa was hospitalized, I was thrilled with his response as I read through the Psalms. He often repeated them with me. Chuck occasionally leads the worship services at Lambeth House. Papa typically repeats the Scriptures aloud with Chuck, and he often shouts "Amen" in response to favorite verses. His lack of inhibitions embarrasses Mom Kelley, but it reminds us that Papa has hidden the Word of God in his heart.

Even though communication abilities change as loved ones age, continued conversation is important to the relationship.

Improved Communication

While there are many areas of lifelong learning, communication is one skill that should be worked on throughout life. As the parent-child relationship develops, mother and daughter must improve their communication with each other. Christians are particularly responsible for enhancing their interaction with others. Biblical advice is given about communication throughout Scripture. Ephesians 4:15, 25–32 offers specific suggestions to improve communication:

- Speak the truth in love (verses 15, 25).
- Control angry words (verse 26).
- Speak words of encouragement and healing (verse 29).
- Avoid unkind or bitter speech (verse 29).
- Speak words of forgiveness (verse 32).

Though it is challenging, Christians can learn to communicate more effectively as they grow in faith and receive power from the Holy Spirit.

I have been consciously working to improve communication with my mothers. As our relationships mature, I have learned some valuable lessons about communicating with others, especially those who are aging. Let me share these personal suggestions in the form of commandments. While they are more practical than biblical, these strategies may also help you communicate more effectively with your mother.

10 Commandments for Communication

1. Thou shalt set a regular time for conversation with your mother. Though daily and weekly schedules may vary, it is helpful to have a specific time for your mother-daughter talks. She can anticipate your call, and you can control the time. I routinely call my mother on Monday mornings as I am driving for my weekly errands. Driving time is a great time for me to multitask, and she is at home getting her week started. Find a time suitable for both of you to talk regularly.

2. Thou shalt think from her perspective when communicating your ideas. Try to consider her values and opinions, even if they differ from yours. Putting yourself in her shoes may minimize conflict and enhance communication. With my mother-in-law, I try hard to listen to what she is saying. I have learned to ask questions to gain information and remember responses from previous discussions. I try my best to understand her, then help facilitate her desires.

3. Thou shalt not take her comments personally. It is true that older people often speak their minds too freely. They may think their age excuses their frankness. Some personalities are more direct than others. Be careful not to take the things your mother says to you too personally. Take the comments at face value, and do not read more into them than is intended. My husband is often concerned by comments my mother makes to me. He loves me and thinks I am perfect, so he will get frustrated with her statements that seem critical of me. I understand my mother and have learned to depersonalize her words and listen for the important facts.

4. Thou shalt not be in a hurry when talking with her. Allow your mother time to talk. While busy schedules are a reality of caregiving daughters, keep in mind your mother's need and desire to talk. I have explained to my moms that sometimes I am in a hurry and sometimes I have time to talk without time pressures. With that fact in mind, I try to begin my phone call or respond to hers with a statement about the time I have available. It helps us both to know how much detail to include and when to delay lengthier conversations.

5. Thou shalt consider her emotions when talking.
Serious discussions should always take place in a quiet, confidential setting. When the time comes to discuss serious topics, try to set aside a time and place for open and honest expression of feelings without time constraints. Chuck and I carefully considered when and where to initiate the conversation with Mom Kelley about moving. Papa needed skilled nursing care, so a move was inevitable. While we had a general conversation by phone, Chuck and I flew to Texas to have that serious discussion with her face-to-face. The three of us sat comfortably in her den and talked openly about the future without concern for time. We laughed and cried freely in that intimate setting. Be sensitive to your mother's feelings and talk privately when possible.

6. Thou shalt listen with interest before giving advice.
Remember how you felt about your mother's unsolicited advice when you were a teenager. Be cautious about offering your own counsel without listening to her concerns and waiting for her solicitation of your opinion. I try not to express my ideas before listening to hers. In fact, I often respond to my mother's questions with, "What do you think?" When appropriate, it is best for mothers to make their own decisions and children to reinforce them.

7. Thou shalt clarify concerns with some concrete evidence. When you have hesitations about their decisions, gather some information together that will justify your concerns. Thoughtful consideration and careful investigation will help mothers make wise choices. When the Kelleys moved to New Orleans, we discussed what to do with their car. Chuck and I felt it was time for Mom Kelley to stop driving, but we didn't want to make that decision for her. She wanted to continue driving. However, when we presented the advantages and disadvantages of driving, she made the decision to sell her car. While she misses the independence of driving, Mom Kelley knows she made the right decision at the right time.

8. Thou shalt write things down to remember them later. It is impossible for anyone to remember everything. Taking notes and making lists can be very helpful. Anxiety is relieved and added pressure is released if information is written down. I have learned to make "to do" lists, including errands for my moms. My mind is filled with too many details to remember all things. My mother is wonderful about making a list of the things she wants to talk about with me. She keeps her list by the phone. When I call her and have time to talk, she works down the list. Her list helps both of us.

9. Thou shalt anticipate concerns and questions. When possible, think ahead to help your mother. Future needs are not always predictable, but you can plan ahead for most routines. During the three years the Kelleys have lived in New Orleans, we have learned about their typical needs. Mom Kelley is hesitant to call us for requests since she does not want to be a burden. So we have developed a mental list to anticipate her needs. Instead of asking her, "Do you need anything?" we ask her specific questions: "Do you need coffee? Do you need a check cashed? Do you need anything at the pharmacy?" By anticipating her future needs and giving her options, we often avoid an emergency need or personal inconvenience.

10. Thou shalt involve others for conversation when you are unavailable. Since communication is so important to parents, children are wise to plan for conversations even in their absence. Interaction with other people encourages the health and happiness of your mother. Since Chuck and I travel often, we have enlisted a number of friends to keep in touch with "the moms." My mother gets out a lot, but Mom Kelley spends most of her time at Lambeth House. While Chuck and I were overseas for several weeks last summer, we developed a schedule for family members or friends to take Mom Kelley out to lunch at least once a week. She initially protested her need to be entertained, but she thoroughly enjoyed the social interaction. The restaurant food was delicious, but it was the conversation with friends that delighted her.

These guidelines have been helpful to Chuck and me as we relate to our mothers. Undoubtedly, there are many other practical suggestions for improving communication. **The key is to keep talking.** Keep the lines of communication open. Keep in touch often by talking and writing.

Written communication cannot be overlooked. While mothers and daughters may often live nearby, many families are separated by the miles. Letters and emails provide excellent communication. Written communication can be read and re-read. It can be shared easily with others. The Kelleys' daughter Kathy has always lived far away from them, but she has faithfully written them a letter every week. They look forward to her mail and share her news with the rest of the family.

Years ago, Mom Kelley began writing a weekly letter to keep in touch with her children. Since she types her letter on pink stationery, the family lovingly refers to it as "the pink letter." In her letters, Mom Kelley carefully describes her own activities as well as the "comings and goings" of others. Her letters keep the family members connected. The children love to receive her weekly letters, and her grandchildren have asked to receive them too. One of the Kelley daughters has begun a regular letter to continue the tradition of family communication. Eileen's efforts are greatly appreciated. It is important for us to keep in touch since the Kelley kids are separated by many miles. Continued conversation and improved communication are essential to meaningful relationships, especially for daughters caring for their aging mothers. It is also important to consider healthy dialogue.

Healthy Dialogue

The difference between monologue and dialogue is obvious. While monologue involves one person talking to herself, dialogue requires two people to exchange ideas, taking turns talking. Since some people are more talkative, they seem to enjoy ongoing monologue. They like to talk and hear themselves talking. However, dialogue is needed for healthy communication. Two people build the relationship with each other as they interact in conversation. As adults grow older, the ability to sustain conversation decreases. Two-way dialogue with aging loved ones often declines into a one-dimensional monologue. Severe communication breakdowns may develop as the years pass and cognition declines.

It is helpful to recognize that your mother may no longer be able to carry on a conversation. Lack of communication may distance the relationship and make caregiving difficult. Try to understand your loved one's language weaknesses. Some senior adults experience communication disorders due to strokes or other neurological impairments. Most older adults face some degree of change in their ability to communicate.

Communication problems that often afflict older adults include comprehension problems and inability to adequately express thoughts. These problems exist in isolation or combination, vary in severity, and often progress over time. Comprehension problems affect the ability to understand what is spoken or read. Words are heard or seen, but correct meaning is not attached to the words. Memory weaknesses are common. Expression problems hinder the ability to put thoughts into coherent words. Words may be spoken without order or meaning. Loved ones must recognize these communication changes and try to adjust to them.

Comprehension problems interfere with a healthy dialogue. The impaired person is unable to understand the message spoken, and therefore is unable to respond appropriately. Lack of understanding can be mistaken for uncooperative behavior. Information may be quickly forgotten. Comprehension of verbal language and written information may be impaired. Your loved one may recognize printed words but not know their meanings. Telephone communication may be challenging since the older adult does not benefit from nonverbal cues, such as facial expressions and gestures used by the speaker.

In their book *The 36-Hour Day*, Mace and Rabins present several helpful suggestions for caregivers communicating with a person who has comprehension problems (pages 38–39). These practical tips may be helpful to you:

1. Make sure the person hears you. Hearing acuity declines in later life and many older people may not hear what is said due to a hearing deficit. Encourage them to consider getting a hearing aid if hearing problems persist.

2. Lower the tone (pitch) of your voice. High frequencies are most often impaired in older people. A lower pitch is easier for them to hear. Speak in a lower tone, not a lower volume.

3. Eliminate distracting noises or activities. Hearing loss and the inability to sort out words from background noises may interfere with your parent's ability to focus and understand. Try to control distractions in the environment.

4. Use short words and simple sentences. Complex statements may overwhelm and confuse the person with comprehension problems. Do not use baby talk with your parents, but do use "simple talk" with them.

5. Ask only one question or present only one task at a time. Multiple questions or multiple instructions may overload their decision-making ability. Break down the questions, and give one command at a time. Short commands and simple questions will increase comprehension and decrease frustration.

6. Speak slowly and wait for the person to respond. No need to shout. Deliberate speech helps a senior adult comprehend as her response times slow down. Deliberate speech also improves the speaker's articulation and clarity.

There are many things you can do to improve communication with your loved one who has comprehension problems. You can also facilitate her ability to express herself. In the case of severe communication disorders, consultation with a speech pathologist is recommended. Professionals can diagnose the type and severity of communication disorder. They can provide speech therapy to remediate comprehension, expression, and memory problems. Speech pathologists can work directly with the senior adults and confer with their caregivers.

It was my joy to work as a speech pathologist for 18 years. I saw many patients improve their skills or learn to compensate as a result of speech therapy. I also watched as many families were successfully involved in the rehabilitation process. Support groups for patients with communicative disorders are also productive. You and your loved one can benefit from therapeutic intervention.

Expressive problems also interfere with healthy dialogue. It is not uncommon for senior adults to have trouble putting their thoughts into words. Some people with expressive language problems have difficulty finding words. They may have trouble remembering names of familiar objects or people. Some people talk fluently, but their thoughts ramble. Older people with language weaknesses may deny their problems or become frustrated. In some cases, profanity is spoken, though often without deliberate intent. Severe verbal language problems challenge communication between the senior adult and caregiver. Patience and empathy are needed by both the impaired speaker and the listener.

Consider these suggestions when talking with your loved one who has expressive language problems.

1. Wait patiently and courteously for the thought to be expressed. Assist only after allowing time for the person to give communication a try. Many senior adults communicate best in a relaxed, calm atmosphere.

2. Provide the word before your loved one becomes frustrated. If you do not know what is intended, ask her to describe or point to the object. Ignore the comment or change the subject if she becomes upset.

3. Carefully consider the context of the person's comments. Meaning can often be clarified by previous or following statements, as well as the environmental setting or nonverbal cues. When possible, try to guess the subject if she becomes upset.

4. Try distracting your loved one when she repeats the same thing over and over. Repetition is common among older adults. Talk about other things or ask questions about the repeated statement. Understand that repetitive conversation is a part of cognitive decline.

5. If the verbal output of your loved one is limited to single words or if communication is only nonverbal, ask simple questions that can be answered with one word or a gesture. Effort and creativity are necessary if your loved one has a severe language problem.

6. When a person cannot communicate, establish a system for determining needs. Anticipate problems and check for comfort. Continue to talk to your nonverbal loved one, who will be encouraged by your presence and voice whether or not she understands you or can talk to you.

Our Papa has communication problems. He has difficulty understanding others and expressing himself. Chuck and I have tried to adapt to his new communication needs. We speak clearly and simply to him. We discuss familiar topics and repeat ourselves often to increase his understanding. We try to listen respectfully as his thoughts and words ramble. We gather meaning from the context of his comments. Within about five minutes, the topic of his verbal perseveration becomes apparent. We try to distract him when his thoughts get stuck, and we often ignore his erroneous comments. While communication with Papa has changed, Chuck and I keep talking to him to maintain our relationship. He obviously loves to talk. His face lights up, and his level of alertness improves when loved ones talk with him.

A church friend is caring for her mother, who has Alzheimer's. Her communication skills are decreasing and causing frustration for everyone. As the primary caregiver, my friend recognizes the challenges and responds accordingly. Read her account below to learn two techniques for communicating more effectively with your loved one as communication problems develop.

Mainly with Mom, there is a communication challenge because she does not understand much of what people tell her verbally. Frequently, my communication with her evolves into high drama. I'm not sure how long that will work, but it is a method that is about 70% effective now. Another way that I communicate with her is by writing her a note. This method is about 95% effective and is a preferred method. It's logistically difficult, though, to leave a conversation with her and type or print a note to her.

Mother gets fixated on something and will not drop it. It is frustrating beyond words. And she will not take my word at face value. She has to get at least one other person to give her the same information before she believes me. For instance, recently I volunteered us for Vacation Bible School. Ever since that week, she has insisted that we are supposed to be at Vacation Bible School. I have told her continually that VBS is over. Last week, she saw another VBS worker at church and came home to announce that Kelly said we were supposed to be at VBS. Of course, Kelly hadn't said that and Mother didn't understand what she did say. So communication with her can be very frustrating!

It is impossible to overemphasize the importance of communication in the mother-daughter relationship. While communication is a significant part of all human relationships, interaction between mother and daughter is critical, especially as the years pass. Daughters must seek to maintain communication even when it is not reciprocated by their mothers. Seek to continue conversation, improve communication, and engage in healthy dialogue with your mother. Time and effort are required for talking. However, the investments are worthwhile. Both mother and daughter benefit from effective interaction. Blessings are abundant as loved ones discuss past memories, present challenges, and future promises.

Mother-Daughter Reflections

1. What Scriptures challenge you about the importance of communication? How do you apply these biblical principles to conversations with your mother?

2. How much time do you spend talking with your mother? Set some goals for continued conversation.

3. What specific strategies will you employ to improve communication with your mother? Write them down, then try to utilize them.

4. Does your mother have some communication challenges? Identify her weaknesses in verbal comprehension and expression so you can communicate more effectively.

5. Consider your last conversation with your mother. Did you talk openly, lovingly, and respectfully? Ask the Lord to help you communicate with your mother in a Christlike manner.

10 Commandments for Communicating with Your Aging Mother

1. Thou shalt set a regular time for conversation with your mother.
2. Thou shalt think from her perspective when communicating your ideas.
3. Thou shalt not take her comments personally.
4. Thou shalt not be in a hurry when talking with her.
5. Thou shalt consider her emotions when talking.
6. Thou shalt listen with interest before giving advice.
7. Thou shalt clarify concerns with some concrete evidence.
8. Thou shalt write things down to remember them later.
9. Thou shalt anticipate concerns and questions.
10. Thou shalt involve others for conversation when you are unavailable.

Communication Tips for Comprehension Problems

1. Make sure the person hears you.
2. Lower the tone (pitch) of your voice.
3. Eliminate distracting noises or activities.
4. Use short words and simple sentences.
5. Ask only one question or present only one task at a time.
6. Speak slowly and wait for the person to respond.

Communication Tips for Expressive Language Problems

1. Wait patiently and courteously for the thought to be expressed.
2. Provide the word before your loved one becomes frustrated.
3. Carefully consider the context of the person's comments.
4. Try distracting your loved one when she repeats the same thing over and over.
5. If the verbal output of your loved one is limited to single words or if communication is only nonverbal, ask simple questions that can be answered with one word or a gesture.
6. When a person cannot communicate, establish a system for determining needs.

Chapter Seven

Facilitating Family Dynamics

The family is a creation of God. His plan for family began as God made man and woman in His image and for His pleasure. In due time and according to His will, Adam and Eve had two sons, adding to their family unit (Genesis 4:1–2). Through their lineage and throughout history, families continue to be a part of God's divine design. The family is an important institution of Almighty God and is a support to each family member. Over time, however, society has distorted God's image of family.

Family is simply defined as "a group of individuals living under one roof and usually under one head" (*Merriam-Webster*,

1997). Individuals form a family unit to provide love and support for each other. The American view of family has changed over time. In the past, a typical family was composed of a father, mother, two children, and a dog. Television portrayed the American family through programs like *Leave It to Beaver* and *Ozzie and Harriet*. Today's worldview of family is different. Nuclear families include various combinations of people, no longer following the biblical model. The media projects a different type of family. There is a new Ozzie on television—Ozzy Osbourne. Families are depicted on TV programs like *The Osbournes* and *The Simpsons*.

Christians are challenged by the worldview of family and must follow God's view. In the beginning, when God created man and woman, He created family as the first human institution. From Genesis through Revelation, God's plan for family was revealed. Family dynamics must be considered, especially as the patriarch and matriarch of the family age.

The Old Testament is filled with many references to and instructions for the family. In Genesis, members of the family are introduced individually—father, mother, and children (Genesis 2:24; 3:20; 17:4). In Exodus, the commandments set parameters for behavior within a family or group of people (Exodus 20). In Numbers, the numbering of the people is accomplished according to family units (Numbers 4:1–2). Deuteronomy emphasizes the role of parental instruction (Deuteronomy 6:1–12), and Joshua describes the godly patriarch who led his family to follow Yahweh (Joshua 24:15). Judges records the impact of Samson's sinful behavior on his family (Judges 16:25–31), while the Book of Ruth portrays the strength of family (Ruth 1:16–17).

In the Books of Samuel, Kings, and Chronicles, the history of Israel notes the influence of the home upon kings. In Ezra, Nehemiah, and Esther, a godly seed was preserved through death, disease, poverty, and internal strife. Psalms contains promises for the home (Psalm 127), while Proverbs and Ecclesiastes abound with maxims about family relationships. The Song of Solomon proclaims the power of love between man and woman in marriage (Song of Solomon 4:1–7). The prophetic books of the Old Testament allude to the open violation of godly principles in families (Isaiah 3:12–26; Lamentations 4:10; Ezekiel 16:44–45; Micah 7:5–6; Malachi 2:13–16).

The New Testament extends and expands God's priority on family. The Gospel of Matthew begins by introducing Jesus, "the Son of David, the Son of Abraham," in terms of family. The virgin Mary was "pregnant by the Holy Spirit" and gave birth to Jesus, the Son of God, the savior of the world (Matthew 1:18, 25). The Gospels present the family of Jesus as well as His teachings about family. In John, Jesus is called the "only begotten Son, who is in the bosom of the Father," and He often refers to Himself as the "Son of God" (John 1:18, 34; 3:18; 9:35; 10:36 NKJV). The Book of Acts includes the home along with the temple as a place for worship and instruction (Acts 2:46; 12:12). The New Testament epistles are full of teachings about the family (1 Corinthians 11:1–16; Ephesians 5:22–6:4; Colossians 3:18–21; 1 Timothy 3:1–5; Titus 2:1–5; Hebrews 12:5–11; 1 Peter 3:1–7).

Surely one of the Bible's most powerful teachings about the family is recorded in John 3:1–21. Those who trust Jesus as personal Savior are described as members of the family of God. God is the Father of all who believe, and we are His children. Each believer becomes a part of the greater family of God at the time of salvation. When we are born, we become children of an earthly father and mother, a part of a biological family. When we are reborn at salvation, believers become children of the heavenly Father, a part of a spiritual family.

Family is undoubtedly important to God and to each member of the family. As Christian members of God's family and our earthly families, we must learn how to follow His purposes and live in harmony with each other. According to Scripture, family members are to love one another, respect one another, and care for one another. Obedience to God's plan for family not only accomplishes His will but also meets many human needs. Family is always important, but it is never more important than in a person's later years.

Family Interaction

As time passes, the family dynamics change. Members of the family need to work together to facilitate healthy interaction. As parents age, it is helpful for family members to support each other and share information in order to promote the best decisions for parents. Effective facilitation of family dynamics involves family interaction, family education, and family support.

People, and thus families, interact in different ways. Interactions are influenced by individual personalities, assumed roles, and geographical location. A father and mother introduce into the family their own personalities and backgrounds. Each child, even though she is birthed by the same parents and raised in the same home, has a unique personality or combination of character traits. It is true that no two children are alike. My sister has 16-year-old twin boys. Aaron and Brent could not be any more unlike each other. While Aaron is athletic and quiet, Brent is musical and social. God has given each of His children a unique personality. Family interactions with different personalities may pose challenges, but they also produce blessings.

Personality differences are seen clearly in the Kelley family. Chuck's parents have unique but complementary personalities.

114

While his dad has always been positive, outgoing, and adventuresome, Chuck's mother tends to be more cautious and conservative. Each of his four sisters has distinctive personalities, though they have some similar traits and values. Chuck would say he has the only perfect personality in his family, though his sisters might disagree! The Kelley kids learned how to adjust to other personalities as they learned to get along together as family.

The family unit is the first small group to which a person ever belongs. Therefore, one purpose of the family is to teach its members how to relate to other people. Interpersonal relationship skills are first learned in the home and continue to be developed throughout life. Individuals learn to negotiate differences as they work to get along with family members.

As parents grow older and need help from others, it is essential for family members to work together, adjusting to each personality. Different personalities respond to the aging process in different ways, and different personalities assume caregiving responsibilities in different ways. Children should work together to support their parents even when their viewpoints differ. Cooperation is definitely God's plan for families.

The interaction of family members is also influenced by the role of each person. Birth order of children continues to affect interaction with parents and siblings. The older and younger children usually assume the same roles in the family throughout life. Gender of siblings also impacts the family dynamics. Sons typically inherit leadership roles in the family, while daughters step into caregiving roles. As parents become more dependent, the roles of children must become more clearly identified. It is important to agree with the roles of family members and work in harmony. Family dynamics are often strained when siblings vie for another child's role.

Family meetings are needed to discuss the roles of children as parents grow older. It is helpful for the family to agree on some guidelines. One child needs to assume the role of power of attorney, ideally one who lives near the parents. One child should become primary caregiver, while other children will play supportive roles. When possible, parents should be included in the family discussions and should have input about which children will fulfill each role.

Geographical location often determines the roles adult children will perform. Children who live near their parents will naturally have more active roles in caregiving. Those who live distances away will assume less active roles and provide periodic care. Each role is important within the family, and no one role is *more* important within the family. Family members who understand their roles and fulfill their responsibilities promote healthier and happier family dynamics. Families that are spread apart geographically must work together even more diligently to maintain good family interaction.

The Kelley family has clearly defined our roles as Papa and Mom Kelley have begun to lean on us for support. Papa is totally dependent on others for his care, though Mom Kelley is fairly independent with only minimal support needed from others. Chuck, their only son, has taken on the role as their power of attorney, helping them make business and medical decisions. Since their move to New Orleans three years ago, I have become their primary caregiver (or "primary care agent," as I have mentioned before). Because they live in other states, the four daughters assume supportive roles. They talk to their parents regularly, visit them often, and help when needed. It strengthens our family dynamics to have these roles clearly understood.

I realize how blessed I am with good family dynamics. Though we encounter occasional differences, for the most part, members of my family get along well together, as do members of Chuck's family. A friend recently shared with me the difficult relationship she and her husband had with his sister. Though they were primary caregivers of their aging parents, the sister provided little support. My friend "tried very hard to let his sister know what was happening, but she was indifferent." The sister didn't respond when the parents faced illnesses and rarely called or visited. When the father died, the sister and her husband took over control of their mother's care. Unfortunately, the selfish sister "confiscated her parents' estate and spent the money foolishly."

Not all family dynamics are healthy and happy. But all family relationships are worth the effort for the sake of its members. Aging parents are supported by healthy, happy family interaction, and Christians practicing such are following biblical teachings about the home. Facilitating family dynamics is a significant part of caregiving.

Family Education

Healthy families have happy family interactions. They also need to receive relevant education about caring for parents in their later years. As parents grow older and develop more health challenges, adult children should gather information about their medical problems and life-care options. Information should be shared with all family members to promote understanding and cooperation. There are many sources of caregiver education today—professionals, programs, and printed materials. Educational Web sites can provide information, and online chat rooms can provide support.

In many ways, I feel that I have become an expert in the field of gerontology or adult caregiving. I have listened to professionals discuss their care of my parents. I have participated in programs designed to educate my parents. I have read about the needs of older people and support systems available to caregivers. It is my responsibility as a daughter and daughter-in-law to share that information with our siblings and others. Information gathered is not intended for storage but for sharing.

Discussing care options is another part of family education. As their needs increase, parents must receive more outside care. Once their needs are identified, family members must ensure that their needs are met. Typically, a combination of services provides for physical, mental, and social needs. Possible services and care options must be discussed with the family initially and continually.

Proper education of a family about elder care will promote healthier family dynamics as well as better care of their loved ones. Members of a larger family will often share responsibilities for education and care. The division of labor can strengthen the parent, support the primary caregiver, and involve the other siblings. Sometimes aging adults without children depend on other family members or friends for caregiving. Children with no siblings may have the sole responsibility of aging parents.

Becky, my dad's wife, is an only child. She recently assumed sole responsibility of both her parents as their health declined. Her mother was diagnosed with Alzheimer's disease and needed full-time care. Her father's health problems increased, so he was no longer able to care for his wife and needed care himself. Becky found herself providing constant care for her parents as they experienced one crisis after another. Housing decisions, hospital stays, and treatment choices overwhelmed her in the last year of their lives. By the grace of God and with the help of medical professionals, Becky was able to gather information, assess care options, and assume responsibility for her parents. It was an intensely stressful but immensely rewarding time in her life. Becky cared for her parents loving-ly until they died, only days apart.

Since Chuck and I have no children of our own, we will be dependent upon others as we age. Of course, we are trying to prepare financially for retirement, and we are making person-al decisions about our own long-term care. However, we love to tease our nephews that they will one day care for us. We also make pacts with friends to take care of each other in our old age. Our future is a serious matter for consideration. We do need to have honest conversations with our family about our wishes for the future. Families need to share information with each other as they care for loved ones.

Family Support

Family interaction and education are precursors to family sup-port. Members of a family can provide needed support for other family members. Everyone needs the help; whether in ongoing assistance or crisis intervention, we need the support of others. The family is a natural support system. While brothers and sisters often support each other in the biological family, brothers and sisters in the Lord should care for each other as well. God's family should be a caregiving family.

One of my sister's 16-year-old twin sons was recently injured at football camp. Because of the severity of Aaron's lacerated kidney, he spent several nights in the ICU, followed by several more days in the hospital and three weeks at home confined to bed rest. Our family rallied to Mitzi's support at her time of crisis. Mother immediately went to the hospital in a city four hours away form New Orleans. She supported Mitzi while Aaron was in ICU. I followed two days later, supporting Mitzi and sitting with Aaron in the hospital. When he was released to go home for convalescence, Mother stayed with Aaron and helped in their home so Mitzi could return to work and get her other sons started in school. Family members are to support each other as needs arise.

A great vehicle for support within a family is consensus building. Family members are strengthened to face life challenges when they are of "like mind." While different opinions are inevitable and diverse desires will develop, members of a family must learn to reach a unified consensus. Give and take may be required. But when all family members agree, there is tremendous support. Consensus building definitely strengthens the family—each member individually and the unit as a whole.

Our friend Joy became the primary caregiver for her parents. She and her brothers had different viewpoints about caregiving, and the boys were not very close to their parents. So Joy carried most of the burden of care, even though she had a young child and lived hundreds of miles away. She had little interaction with her brothers because of their differences. But Joy felt blessed to support her parents. She "learned a great deal from them, grew as a Christian, and grew personally" as she provided for her parents. God was faithful and Joy survived! God does bless His children who care for their loved ones.

Inevitably, conflict will arise within the family. Different opinions and unclear communication will cause friction. For the sake of parents and in obedience to the Lord, adult children must resolve their conflicts. Small disputes should not be ignored or they will develop into major conflicts. Communication and compromise will facilitate healthy family dynamics and provide helpful support. Frequent interactions and sibling cooperation are worth the time and effort invested in conflict management.

Constant communication is an obvious means of support for the family. Keeping in touch by phone or email as well as through periodic visits and letters will improve communication within the family and provide support to all members. (See chapter 6, "Maintaining Communication," for a thorough discussion of this topic.) Each member of the family should try to communicate clearly and continually to facilitate family dynamics and foster better care of parents.

The family is a strong source of love and support. God's desire is for His children to develop a sense of belonging and acceptance of responsibility within the family. Mutual help and encouragement are experienced by family members over time. As parents age, adult children provide more support and together the challenges of the later years are met.

In her book *The Family: Unchanging Principles for Changing Times* (pages 179–180), my sister-in-law Dorothy Patterson concludes: "Families are the earthly vessel through which a mother and father and their children can bind themselves together in loving devotion and face whatever may come with confidence that with one another and the Lord they can indeed overcome the obstacles of life and find happiness."

How true! Family members develop an indescribable bond that connects them together for life. They provide support for each other in times of need. As parents face their final years, devoted children help them overcome the obstacles of life and find happiness. Though family dynamics may at times be difficult, the blessings of family are worth the work.

Mother-Daughter Reflections

1. Who is your family? Take a few minutes to think about the people who make up your immediate and extended family. Thank the Lord for each of them!

2. What have been the best sources of education about elder care for you and your family?

3. Consider the personalities of your immediate family members. How do they affect your interactions?

4. How do you support your family? What role do you fulfill with your parents?

5. How do the biblical teachings about family impact your interactions with your family?

Chapter Eight

Nurturing Reconciliation

I nevitably, families will at some time experience relationship problems. Misunderstandings develop and miscommunication occurs, causing tension between parents and children or among siblings. Numerous examples of family discord are available in the world. Well-known actors and actresses acknowledge estrangement from their parents. Famous siblings fuss and feud publicly. Tension builds in those relationships.

Unfortunately, Christians also encounter differences with members of their families. Even though the Bible teaches about harmony in relationships, human nature causes Christians to hold grudges and assign blame. Small disagreements become huge arguments. Hurt feelings lead to strong bitterness. Tensions escalate and relationships are broken. In these circumstances, God must convince the Christian of ungodly behavior and encourage forgiveness of all transgressions. Relationships can be reconciled with the help of the Holy Spirit, and restoration can occur.

Have you and your family experienced any broken relationships? Have you and your parents encountered serious differences? Have you and your siblings faced personal tensions? It is healthy to resolve conflict at any time, but it is especially important to right any wrongs as your parents age. More than ever before, families must unite to care for each other.

This chapter will consider restoring, reconciling, and rebuilding relationships. Once issues of difference and feelings of hurt have been recognized, a Spirit-led Christian can reconcile with others and rebuild relationships. There is great joy in happy homes, and there is tremendous support in harmonious families.

Restoring Relationships

Families are not exempt from broken relationships. In fact, because they live together and must relate regularly with each other, families may develop more tensions than do other relationships. Relatives are unable to ignore differences for long since interaction is more frequent. Families must recognize problems and restore healthy relationships. Families throughout human history have failed to restore broken relationships and have been hurt by painful experiences.

Family feuds have developed within families and between families. In the Bible, family conflicts were described between Cain and Abel, as well as between Jacob and Esau, among others. Cain killed Abel out of anger and vengeance (Genesis 4:1–15). The twins Esau and Jacob began fighting in Rebekah's womb and continued fighting until Esau sold his birthright to his brother Jacob (Genesis 25:19–34).

In literature and history, family feuds are recorded. *Romeo and Juliet*, a tragic play by William Shakespeare, depicted hatred between two families. Violence and hatred developed between the Montagues and Capulets and resulted in the deaths of five loved ones before the parents stopped their feuding. In American history, a full-blown family feud ignited between the Hatfields and McCoys in the late 19th century. The fight over stolen hogs and timber prices led two families to court, then to battle. The family feud continued for six years and resulted in many deaths. Dysfunctional family relationships are not healthy for any of the people involved.

Several factors may lead to broken relationships within families. These factors include but are not limited to

- disagreements
- distrust
- divorce
- distance

All of these contribute to friction among family members. Let's briefly discuss each one.

Disagreements occur when loved ones have different perspectives, different priorities, or different personalities. It is natural for disagreements to arise since every family member is unique. But disagreements must be acknowledged, then accepted. Differences are simply differences and should be respected. Family members should learn how to handle disagreements through communication, compromise, and cooperation.

Distrust develops when family members betray confidences, tell lies, or fail to follow through on promises. People who have been previously hurt become skeptical and overly cautious. Defenses arise as a protective mechanism against future disappointment. Time and forgiveness are needed to rebuild trust.

Divorce also causes division in families. When parents or their adult children divorce, family members may take sides with one person and blame the other. Divorce impacts all members of the family, not just the couple. And since divorce rates, even among Christian marriages, continue to rise, family tensions increase. Unconditional love and unbroken connection must continue within a family even after divorce.

Distance is another factor that challenges families. Many families are separated by miles. Extended families rarely live in close proximity to one another. Geographical distance can lead to relational distance. Even though relational distance is undesired, it is inevitable. Busy lives and hectic schedules contribute to the lack of family time. Family members must work to stay in contact with each other. Each one must prioritize communication and plan for visits.

Distance is the greatest challenge that our families face. While Chuck and I are blessed to live in the same town as our parents, our siblings are scattered around the country. We must work hard to stay in touch. When tensions develop within the family, the obvious cause is distance. When we fail to prioritize family visits, phone calls, and letter writing, our families seem divided and disagreements may develop.

One of our friends always seems to be having a family drama. Her parents and the children often seem to have disagreements. Distrust has developed among them through the years. One adult child is again facing divorce, and her marital problems are causing friction within the family. Though all family members once lived in the same town, the family is now separated by distance. Their family dysfunction has hurt each family member. But relationships can be restored if each person will forgive and work together in love.

Reconciling Relationships

Broken relationships are inevitable in any family, but reconciliation is possible through the power of the Holy Spirit. Reconciliation can be simply defined as "a change from enmity to friendship" (*WebBible Encyclopedia*). The New Testament teaches that reconciliation began at the cross. Through Christ's death on the cross, God reconciled the world to Himself (2 Corinthians 5:18). Sinful human beings are no longer His enemies but His children; enmity is transformed into friendship. Jesus Christ can also help His children reconcile with one another.

Reconciliation is both objective and subjective. By His grace, God chooses to reconcile sinners to Himself. By human choice, sinners can accept His gift and be reconciled in faith. Christians must also choose to be reconciled with others. Past disappointments and painful injustices must be put behind so that enmity can be transformed into friendship. All relationships need reconciliation, and families will survive only if they are reconciled. Reconciliation in families is always desired, but it is desperately needed as parents age. Without reconciliation, death brings added pain. Several truths about reconciliation are taught in Scripture and exemplified by the life of Jesus.

In order to be reconciled with loved ones, Christians must extend **undeserved forgiveness.** No one deserves forgiveness. Forgiveness is granted by God as an act of mercy and grace. Therefore, Christians must decide to forgive all people, whether or not they deserve forgiveness. Families can often be reunited and differences can be mended when one person offers undeserved forgiveness. While wounded loved ones may not "feel" like forgiving the accused, obedience to God involves volitional forgiveness. Forgiveness must be offered so that reconciliation can begin. In fact, the Bible teaches that forgiveness of others is a prerequisite for receiving God's forgiveness. In the Lord's Prayer, Jesus prayed, "Forgive us our sins, for we ourselves also forgive everyone in debt to us" (Luke 11:4). Family members must offer undeserved forgiveness to each other.

In addition to undeserved forgiveness, reconciliation involves **unconditional love.** True love is unconditional, not dependent on another person's actions. The love of God is expressed to all people, no matter what their commitment to God. Christians are commanded to "love the Lord your God with all your heart" and "love your neighbor as yourself" (Matthew 22:37–40). Love is the great commandment. God's love for us is the model for our love for others. His love is unconditional. Families must love the Lord and love each other without condition; then reconciliation can take place.

Unending compromise is also essential to reconciliation. Individuals involved in conflict should not compromise their convictions or beliefs. Instead, compromise of *opinions* and *desires* is needed for reconciliation. Family members must be willing to concede arguments and acknowledge wrong. "Give and take" should be practiced. Though most people naturally feel strongly about their opinions, compromise is constructive when loved ones disagree. Unending compromise is needed by parents and children in the later years.

Forgiveness and understanding of past hurts help parents and children reconcile broken relationships. My friend Janet learned this lesson in her relationship with her mother, who had a history of mental illness. At the age of 20, Janet had her first child and was hurt by her mother's feelings of anger and jealousy. Later, Janet understood her mother's illness. She "prayed and asked the Lord to give her love and forgiveness" toward her mother. He did and Janet's change of heart helped her better understand her mother as well as her own children. In fact, that answered prayer has nurtured the extended family's relationships.

Rebuilding Relationships

When family relationships are broken, reconciliation is necessary. When reconciliation takes place, restoration is possible. Family members experience great joy and relief when they rebuild broken relationships. Rebuilding broken relationships is hard work. A broken relationship will never be the same, but relationships that are important can be restored. New relationships and even stronger relationships can develop.

When my father and mother divorced, my relationship with Dad was severed. I was hurt and betrayed by his abandonment and immorality. God convicted me, calling me to forgive my dad and continue loving him. I had to accept the fact that our relationship would never be the same. However, I trusted God to help me build a new relationship with my dad. With the power of the Holy Spirit, I was able to resume communication and rebuild a new relationship with Dad. In many ways, my relationship with my dad today is better than before, even though it is different. Because of our experiences through the years and the lessons I have learned from the Lord, we now have a strong bond of love and understanding.

Rebuilding a family relationship takes time and effort. Three steps are involved: you must restore trust, respond to family needs, and redeem the time left. Though you may often think you are the only person in your family working hard, your work is worth the effort. Not only will restoration bring glory to God, it will also bring joy to your family.

Trust in or dependence on another person is a valuable quality. Confidence in a person builds over time. A person's character and strength help determine whether or not they can be trusted. Christians trust in God by faith. Because of His perfect nature, God is totally trustworthy. People, however, are not always trustworthy. Dishonesty, deceit, and disappointment lead to distrust. Once trust is broken, it is difficult to be restored. Families must learn to trust and depend on each other again and again.

In order to rebuild broken relationships, family members must restore trust and respond to family needs. Personal needs increase as people age and health problems are encountered. Family members can provide significant support to each other in times of need. Though crises are never convenient, family members must prioritize emergencies. Relationships are strengthened when loved ones respond to needs, and relatives will reciprocate when the other faces problems. One blessing of family is the mutual support offered throughout life.

My sister's friend recently told her that she had used all her vacation days going to the podiatrist and urologist with her mother. Her mother's needs had consumed her time off. She is not alone. The recent surge in elder care has found many adult children staying home from work to care for aging parents. In recent years, more employees are using the "Family and Medical Leave Act" to support taking time off from work to care for ailing parents. Companies can expect a rise in work leave to care for the needs of parents. Responding to personal needs is a part of being family and can often be the catalyst for rebuilding a broken relationship.

A final step in the process of rebuilding is redeeming the time. Time is fleeting. Every moment is precious. Family members need to value time together. The future is in God's hands, and life is uncertain. Therefore, families should treasure their times together and work diligently to gather together often. Though it is easy to resent demands on your time as your parents age, you should savor the moments, listen intently to their stories, and spend time in conversation.

Rebuilding is not a fast fix. It is a slow process, an investment in the future. I cannot discuss rebuilding relationships without mentioning the rebuilding that is taking place on the campus of the New Orleans Baptist Theological Seminary at this time. On August 29, 2005, Hurricane Katrina hit the city of New Orleans and the Gulf Coast with high-speed winds. After the levees broke, our 85-acre campus flooded. The water rose to eight feet in places, flooding the first floors of all faculty homes and student housing. While the major buildings on our front block and our President's Home were spared flooding, our campus, like the city of New Orleans, was devastated. At this time, the campus is being rebuilt. The strong foundations and solid frameworks make rebuilding a realistic task. What a great day it will be when our seminary family moves back to our beautiful campus!

Family structures can withstand the challenges of life better when they are built on solid foundations. Families grounded in their faith will be strengthened when they face life's storms. Family tensions are inevitable. When (not if) a feud erupts in your family, keep these practical principles in mind:

1. **Communicate clearly.**
2. **Clarify the situation.**
3. **Understand other opinions.**
4. **Try not to judge.**
5. **Forgive and forget.**
6. **Look for common ground.**
7. **Create boundaries and set limits.**
8. **Compromise for the good.**
9. **Seek third-party input to help work out differences.**
10. **Work hard on the relationship.**

One of our friends is now caring for her mother. Theirs is a difficult relationship because they have been estranged for many years. My friend was three years old when her mother abandoned the family. Throughout her childhood, their only contact was "forced visitation." Since her mother was absent most of her life, they have a very strained, superficial relationship. She still feels hurt and bitterness because of past wrongs. Forgiveness must take place for their relationship to be restored. Forgiveness will be difficult since my friend's pain has multiplied through the years. With the Holy Spirit's help, my friend can forgive and can build a meaningful relationship with her mother.

In an article published in *HomeLife* magazine, Chuck and I shared some biblical principles about forgiveness even when it hurts. These teachings were helpful to us as God convicted us to forgive my father, who had rebelled against the Lord. I pray that the following words of Scripture will help you reconcile any broken relationships.

1. See sin clearly. "But as it is, you boast in your arrogance. All such boasting is evil" (James 4:16).

2. Confront honestly. "If your brother sins against you, go and rebuke him in private" (Matthew 18:15).

3. Grieve personally. "Be angry and do not sin. Don't let the sun go down on your anger, and don't give the Devil an opportunity.... No rotten talk should come from your mouth, but only what is good for the building up of someone in need, in order to give grace to those who hear. And don't grieve God's Holy Spirit, who sealed you for the day of redemption. All bitterness, anger and wrath, insult and slander must be removed from you, along with all wickedness. And be kind and compassionate to one another, forgiving one another, just as God also forgave you in Christ" (Ephesians 4:26–27, 29–32).

4. Wait patiently. "I, therefore, the prisoner in the Lord, urge you to walk worthy of the calling you have received, with all humility and gentleness, with patience, accepting one another in love, diligently keeping the unity of the Spirit with the peace that binds us" (Ephesians 4:1–3).

5. Believe hopefully. "Now finally, all of you should be like-minded and sympathetic, should love believers, and be compassionate and humble, not paying back evil for evil or insult for insult but, on the contrary, giving a blessing, since you were called for this, so that you can inherit a blessing. For the one who wants to love life and to see good days must keep his tongue from evil and his lips from speaking deceit, and he must turn away from evil and do good. He must seek peace and pursue it" (1 Peter 3:8–11).

6. Love unconditionally. "Therefore, God's chosen ones, holy and loved, put on heartfelt compassion, kindness, humility, gentleness, and patience, accepting one another and forgiving one another if anyone has a complaint against another. Just as the Lord has forgiven you, so also you must forgive. Above all, put on love—the perfect bond of unity" (Colossians 3:12–14).

7. Forgive willingly. "For if you forgive people their wrongdoing, your heavenly Father will forgive you as well" (Matthew 6:14).

8. Renew spiritually. "Righteousness and justice are the foundation of Your throne; faithful love and truth go before You. Happy are the people who know the joyful shout; LORD, they walk in the light of Your presence" (Psalm 89:14–15).

9. Reunite joyfully. "How good and pleasant it is when brothers can live together!" (Psalm 133:1).

10. Live victoriously. "I have told you these things so that in Me you may have peace. You will have suffering in this world. Be courageous! I have conquered the world" (John 16:33).

God's Word can encourage and instruct us when our families are in turmoil. Personal misunderstanding will occur, but the Lord can resolve conflicts. Dedicate yourself to your family and commit yourself to restoring broken relationships, reconciling divided relationships, and rebuilding severed relationships. God will be glorified, you will be forgiven, and your loved ones will be blessed.

Mother-Daughter Reflections

1. Has your family experienced broken relationships? Consider the nature of those differences.

2. What has the Bible taught you about reconciling broken relationships?

3. Is there anyone in your family who has lost your trust? Who? How will you rebuild that trust?

4. Have you offered forgiveness to everyone in your family who has wronged you? Why or why not?

5. How can you nurture reconciliation in your family?

Biblical Principles about Forgiveness

1. See sin clearly (James 4:16).
2. Confront honestly (Matthew 18:15–17).
3. Grieve personally (Ephesians 4:26–27, 29–32).
4. Wait patiently (Ephesians 4:1–3).
5. Believe hopefully (1 Peter 3:8–11).
6. Love unconditionally (Colossians 3:12–14).
7. Forgive willingly (Matthew 6:14).
8. Renew spiritually (Psalm 89:14–15).
9. Reunite joyfully (Psalm 133:1).
10. Live victoriously (John 16:33).

Chapter Nine

Fostering Independence

Most humans want independence. They want to have their own desires. They want their wishes fulfilled and they want them right now. A great life struggle is balancing a desire for independence with the need for dependence. All relationships face that tension. God's children want their own way while they know God's ways are best. Children want to do their own thing while parents seek their best interests.

Parents know that they are raising their children to become independent, to live life on their own. Through the years, those children who become adults get very accustomed to their independence. They are responsible for their own actions, and they make their own decisions. As adults become older, their bodies and minds age, making it necessary to depend again on others. It is a tough life lesson to let go of independence and become dependent on other people, but that is the cycle of life.

Most families maintain a good balance of dependence and independence among individual members. However, some families develop an unhealthy overdependence on each other. It is dysfunctional for an adult to become overly dependent on another adult unless there is a disability or medical crisis.

A childhood friend of mine always had an unhealthy dependence upon her parents. Even after she married and had her own children, my friend depended more on her parents emotionally than she did on herself or her husband. This overdependence later affected her marriage and her children. She continues to face serious personal problems because of her unnatural dependence on her parents.

This chapter will consider how to foster independence in aging parents. It is in everyone's best interest for parents to remain as independent as possible for as long as possible. While there are some general guidelines, each individual and each family must make this difficult personal decision. Needs and circumstances vary. There is no ideal solution. Instead, we must seek God's help to know what is best for our loved ones and our families. We must learn patience and cooperation as more support is needed.

My friend at church faced that challenge with her mother who had Alzheimer's disease. She and her siblings were being "pushed by pushy, well-meaning relatives to do something about Mom." When the family asked relatives to help provide support, "those pushy, well-meaning relatives wouldn't show up to take Mom places and she would call in hysterics."

Over time it became apparent that her mother could not live independently, so other arrangements were made. The mother's loss of independence was a huge challenge for the concerned family.

Desired Independence

A recent *Good Housekeeping* article (November 2005) reported the results of a national survey that found that 90% of seniors want to stay in their homes as long as possible. Experts call this phenomenon "aging in place." Older people simply call it their deepest wish—to stay at home. Living at home reflects an individual's basic desire for independence. Aging parents typically want to be on their own and continue living just like they have been living. But declining health often makes that desire for complete independence impossible.

Senior adults express their desire for independence in many ways. Some older parents become hurt and assert, "I am a capable adult." They feel a need to prove themselves of worth and value even when they are aging. Most children recognize the abilities of their parents, yet they want to help meet their needs. It is important for children to affirm their parents while offering assistance and support.

My friend Judi recalled her tremendous admiration for her mother. She "had navigated so much of her life without a supportive husband and had raised children, managing everything pretty well." She recognized her mother's abilities and appreciated her mother for balancing her family's checkbook each month. Judi's challenge was "knowing how much to take over" as her mother's health declined. She realized that her mother was "set in her ways." As Judi became more involved in her mother's life, she "proceeded with care and caution," acknowledging her mother's abilities while supporting her increasing limitations.

Other senior adults become defensive. They protest, "I can take care of myself." Though they are older and sometimes weaker, most older parents are capable of caring for themselves in some areas, even though they are declining in other areas. Children should encourage their parents to provide for their own needs as long as possible. Even smaller tasks give meaning and purpose to life. To the extent possible, children should facilitate their parents living independently.

The recent feature article in *Good Housekeeping* provided practical information to help seniors care for themselves. Adjustments to furniture and additions of adaptive devices can protect parents and assist their function. The special report suggested banisters on stairways, grab bars in tubs, and nonskid floor mats to prevent falls. Specific suggestions were given for common problems of aging: poor nutrition, failing eyesight, hearing loss, and prescribed medication. Simple adjustments in the home can help aging parents take care of themselves longer.

Another concern voiced by senior adults comes basically from the independence promoted by our country. They claim, "I have rights." Their statement is true. All Americans do have rights. We live in a free country with laws protecting our inalienable rights. Fortunately, many laws do prevent seniors from being exploited and others ensure their personal freedoms. Children must affirm the rights of a parent and allow them to exercise their rights when in their best interest.

My sister-in-law Dorothy shared with me one of the challenges of raising parents. She concluded that "perhaps one of the greatest challenges comes in helping parents give up some of what they consider to be their rights and freedoms." While children need to respect their parents' desire for independence, Dorothy suggested that it is best when parents "willingly relinquish some of their own preferences." It helps the family interaction if a parent will "make a choice to allow their children, who have now become their caretakers, to make important decisions for them, after consultation with them."

Senior adults may also complain, saying, "I can make my own decisions." Because they have made decisions for themselves for so long, and they have rarely consulted their children for advice, older parents often feel threatened or smothered when children get involved in their decision making. Open communication helps parents begin discussing their personal business. Options can be considered and family gatherings can become times of dialogue. Children must encourage input by parents and must support their decisions as long as possible. Total assumption of decision making should be made delicately and with care for the loved one's feelings.

My mother is a very wise woman, and she has made many good decisions throughout her lifetime. As she has gotten older, Mother solicits advice from Chuck and me more often as she faces big decisions. We have learned to listen and discuss the options with her, but allow her to make the final decision. Not only is Mother enjoying her independence now, but we are learning her values and preferences to make better decisions for her when she cannot make them for herself.

I will mention one final comment often made by senior adults. In frustration, they frequently announce, "I want to live my own life." While they typically don't mean they don't want to have anything to do with you, they are desperately asserting their desire to live like they used to live. They want some freedom. Mothers often have trouble letting go of their children as they grow up. Grown up children may have trouble letting go of their parents as they age. Children should allow their parents to maintain their own identities and live their own lives when appropriate.

Since aging parents have to give up so much, it is helpful if they can maintain some of their personal interests. My friend Karen told me about her mother's love of baseball.

My mom loves baseball. She is 86 and knows the batting averages and the team rosters for the Astros, Rangers, Braves, and Yankees. Everything stops when those teams are on television. She will talk to the TV and the players, being manager and umpire. She will empathize when they make bad plays or lose, and rejoice when they make good plays. She writes fan letters to various players. When she watches baseball, she is enthusiastic and optimistic.

Karen is encouraging her mother to live her own life and pursue some personal interests, though her needs for support are greater than before.

Inevitable Limitations

Gradually, subtle signs of parental aging are noticed by adult children. While ignored at first, little changes lead to concern. The realities of aging are eventually noticed, and signs of decline cannot be ignored. The passing of time brings about inevitable limitations. While few people embrace aging with glee, all of us must accept aging and recognize changes.

Like most of my peers, I don't feel like my age. I feel much younger than my years. I joke about my 10th anniversary of my 29th birthday. I can't believe it when I tell people I have been married 32 years. And I truly can't believe that I am over 50 and approaching 60. It is also difficult to accept how young the students are at New Orleans Seminary. Age is very relative to me.

My mother is a very youthful, healthy, active 79-year-old. I love telling people her age because she is amazing. I am proud of her vigor and pray for her genes to sustain me. Mother has few personal limitations at this time. However, I am so grateful when she recognizes an obvious limitation. She has acknowledged that she cannot perform physical labor like she used to do, and she also limits her driving at night. She paces her activities during the day and occasionally takes a nap. I am glad that Mother accepts her inevitable limitations as they gradually appear.

Changes due to aging usually progress slowly. Children notice their parents becoming more forgetful or less energetic. Frequent bumps or bruises are seen. Motor weakness and visual impairment become apparent. Sometimes an accident or injury speeds up the decline or advanced age slows down recovery. A previously able-bodied parent may have difficulty getting around. A sharp-minded parent may become confused or inattentive. Life is changing and adjustments are needed.

Some inevitable limitations develop as parents grow older. These include but are not limited to

- health
- memory
- finances
- housing
- transportation

While some senior adults are very healthy, others face chronic health or medical problems. Some have good recall, while others have obvious memory problems. Most people lose immediate recall or short-term memory before losing long-term memory. Financial limitations are often experienced as retirees live on fixed incomes. Housing challenges emerge as less house is needed and cost of living increases. Transportation problems limit activities as the elderly can no longer drive. Many other issues also limit the independence of older adults.

In recent years, more of my friends have expressed concern about their parents' decline. One friend was concerned about her mother-in-law's safety when driving. Another friend was worried about her widowed mother living alone. A third friend often mentions her mother's poor health and frequent hospitalizations. The inevitable limitations of aging gradually become apparent.

I have a dear friend who is in the midst of a crisis with her mother. While her mother has experienced health problems through the years, she has faced sudden cognitive decline. My friend was shocked by her mother's rapid onset of dementia. Though she realized some subtle signs of change, it never dawned on her that her mother may have dementia. As she is overwhelmed by her mother's inevitable limitations, she is also trying to decide how to care for her mother. She must foster some independence while providing adequate support.

None of these concerns are unusual. They are typical characteristics of aging. However, these inevitable limitations can become overwhelming crises when they are experienced by you and your family. Families must learn to accept the inevitable decline of the later years. A tension between independence and dependence develops. But a balance can be maintained when families communicate and resources are consulted.

Healthy Dependence

Families can experience healthy dependence, that perfect combination of personal independence and family support. Healthy dependence involves cooperation between aging parents and their adult children. It develops as a result of collaborative effort and can be maintained until significant change occurs. Families must continue to reestablish healthy dependence. When parents encounter new stages and have greater needs, they should willingly seek additional support from their children. Again, balance must be established in the relationship between parent and child, loved one and caregiver.

The law in the United States clearly identifies a "dependent." A dependent can be claimed as a tax deduction when filing personal income tax returns. A child or a parent is legally dependent when more than half of their financial support is provided for them by a caregiver. Support includes food, clothing, housing, and transportation. Many Americans today can claim their aging parents as a tax deduction if they are providing more than half of their financial support. The future will produce even more elderly dependents and hopefully more benefits for caregivers.

As the years pass, adults inevitably become more dependent. In the meantime, it is ideal to determine a healthy dependence. Not only will the older parent enjoy greater freedom and personal independence, but an adult child will have fewer demands and fewer caregiving responsibilities. Healthy dependence is a desired state of being for family relationships.

To develop and maintain healthy dependence for your parents, you might want to keep these "Dos and Don'ts" in mind.

1. Do provide support. Give of yourself to your parents. Listen, assist, and encourage. People need each other.

2. Don't hover too much. Control your worry and don't become overly protective. Your parents will feel stifled and helpless if you baby them.

3. Do be honest and open. Talk openly with your parents about all matters. Face your own fears about the uncertain future.

4. Don't talk down to them. Even when your parents experience mental decline, don't talk to them like they are children and don't talk about them as if they weren't present.

5. Do seek their input. Encourage them to express their own desires and involve them in decision making for as long as possible.

6. Don't take over their lives. Cooperation, not control, is the key in caring for your aging parents. Remember that God is in control, not you.

7. Do try to fulfill their wishes. Your parents may have deep desires that you may not know about. Try to know their wishes and facilitate them when possible.

8. Don't act burdened by their needs. While care of others is very time consuming, don't complain about the imposition. Set some limits, learn to say no to nonessentials, then enjoy your investment of time.

9. Do be available. Be hands-on in the care of your parents. Don't let financial support substitute for personal support. Get involved and be helpful.

10. Don't spread yourself too thin. Burn out and resentment develop when caregivers do too much and don't care for themselves. Consider your own needs as well as the needs of your mother.

In the article "Caring Across the Miles" by Irene Levine and Betsy Rubiner in *Better Homes and Gardens* (April 2005), the example is given of Kathy Waite, who cared for her mother for ten years. Kathy traveled 500 miles three or four times a year to help her mother. When she could no longer juggle her job, the constant worry, and the eight-hour trips, 58-year-old Kathy took early retirement to live with her mother. She attempted to balance her own needs and her mother's needs for years. As her mother's health declined and she became less independent, Kathy found a new balance. In the later stages of life, her mother remained at home with her daughter's presence. A healthy dependence was determined. Each family must find that unique balance, fostering independence while providing support.

An adult child personally desires independence and dignity. Aging parents also want independence and dignity. One of your most important jobs will be preserving their rights while providing for their needs. Find meaningful ways for your parents to help themselves and others. Focus on others often diminishes feelings of self-pity. You can foster independence in your parents as you understand their desire for independence, recognize inevitable limitations, and establish a healthy dependence.

Mother-Daughter Reflections

1. In what ways do you seek to enjoy your own independence? How does your mother seek her own independence?

2. How do you inhibit your mother's desire for independence? What can you do to change that behavior?

3. What inevitable limitations are you experiencing personally as you age? What limitations is your mother facing?

4. Have you been able to establish the balance between independence and dependence with your parents? Why or why not?

5. What is your mother doing to express her independence by helping others?

Dos and Don'ts of Healthy Dependence

1. Do provide support.
2. Don't hover too much.
3. Do be honest and open.
4. Don't talk down to them.
5. Do seek their input.
6. Don't take over their lives.
7. Do try to fulfill their wishes.
8. Don't act burdened by their needs.
9. Do be available.
10. Don't spread yourself too thin.

Chapter Ten

Encouraging
New Friendships

F riendships are important throughout life. Children love playing with
their best friends. Teenagers spend
hours on the telephone talking with their
best friends. Young adults enjoy taking
trips with their best friends. Even older
adults cherish time spent with friends.
Relationships with those outside the family are important. Older parents, especially
mothers, need a larger circle of friends than
family members to give meaning and
purpose to life.

Carol realizes that her mother has an
even greater need for friendships than she
does herself. She is amazed by her mother's
uncanny ability to remember people for

years. Carol's mother recently went to a wedding and saw a woman she recognized. Though she had not seen her in 60 years, she remembered that they sat close to each other in school. Carol's mother considers people to be very important. "She remembered the lady's name! She remembers every detail about our family—cousins, uncles, aunts—even those we haven't seen in years. She knows them and everything about them."

As the needs of aging parents increase, it may be difficult to justify the time required to promote your parent's social life. You may be so busy assisting with their physical and financial concerns that you don't even think about their need for friends. You may be so busy organizing family gatherings that you haven't given thought to get-togethers with other people. However, older adults benefit from friendships just as younger adults do. Fellowship is uplifting to them.

The desire for friendships among women is obvious in my church. Younger women want to know older women. Older women love being around younger women. Friendships and mentoring relationships may develop spontaneously. In our church, we foster friendships among women. We have responded to the search for friends by developing a mentoring program. One member of our women's ministry team serves as our "Menta Yente." (Remember the matchmaker named Yente in the musical *Fiddler on the Roof?*) Harriet is available to help ladies find friends of other ages among our church membership. As they meet, the two ladies build a relationship that helps meet their need for friendship and mentoring.

The Bible records a woman's need for friends. In the Old Testament, Ruth and Naomi built a strong relationship. Even after the death of Ruth's husband, Mahlon (Naomi's son), their friendship deepened and lasted for a lifetime. Naomi prayed for loving-kindness (Hebrew *checed*) toward her daughter-in-law (Ruth 1:8). In fact, *checed* was a theme of the Book of Ruth. Naomi praised God for His loving-kindness (Ruth 2:20), and later Boaz praised Ruth for her loving-kindness (Ruth 3:10). The friendship between Naomi and Ruth was based on love, loyalty, and commitment.

In the New Testament, the special kinship between Elizabeth and Mary is recorded in Luke chapter 1. Though related as cousins, the women became trusted friends because of their shared faith and common calling. Both were pregnant, carrying sons who would later be messengers of God. Their special friendship must have been encouraging to them personally, and it sets an example for Christian women today.

Just before she sold her home, my mother hosted a series of Christmas teas. While she wanted to extend hospitality, her primary purpose was to get older women and younger women in our church together for fellowship. She carefully sent invitations to the young adult and senior adult Sunday school members. Then, Mother strategically assigned the seating, placing two older women and two younger women at each table. She hosted three Saturday afternoon teas and served about 60 ladies. Each lady had a lovely time. Friendships were started and interaction was enjoyed by everyone, especially Mother.

Women today need the same forever friendships. Your mother needs the love and support of friends. Since you are unable to provide for all her relational needs, you should help her maintain friendships with other women whenever possible. She will be blessed, so will you, and so will others.

Relating Friend to Friend

Friendships typically develop because of common interests and desires. While work is necessary to continue the contact, there must be some initial commonality that connects people.

Think about your dearest friend. How did that friendship begin? What drew you together at first? It was probably a similar interest or common experience.

I am so grateful for many dear friends, women with whom I have shared life. Most of my friendships began during stages of my life when we connected through a mutual experience—childhood neighbors, high school chums, seminary students, or ministers' wives. We got to know each other because we had something in common, then we maintained a relationship through the years. Though my friends all have a very different personalities, we built friendships of mutual love because we walked through life at the same time and in the same way.

In their Bible study *Woman to Woman: Preparing Yourself to Mentor*, Edna Ellison and Tricia Scribner discuss how to develop "heart-core intimacy." They conclude that "heart-core intimacy develops in a relationship when each person translates shared traditions, shared experiences, shared humor, and each person's uniqueness into meaning, not only for the individual, but also for the pair" (page 88). They suggest three ways to establish common ground—share life traditions, life experiences, and spiritual experiences. They also recommend three ways to build a relationship through shared events—making memories, sharing humor, and celebrating uniqueness. Friendship can blossom when two people who relate friend to friend build a close bond through shared interests.

When relationships begin, conversation focuses typically on common ground. Women talk about life traditions, such as family occasions, religious customs, or food preferences. As women discuss these familiar topics, they begin to connect and often build new friendships. New friends may also talk about life experiences—marriage, family, household moves, or illnesses. Conversations among Christian women are often about spiritual experiences, such as personal conversion, ministry calling, or life rededication. Shared events are also favorite topics of conversation that forms deep relationships. People begin to build strong relationships as they share common bonds.

I am so grateful that my mother and Chuck's mother are such good friends. While they have always liked each other, a deep friendship developed when Mom Kelley moved to New Orleans, and my mother also moved to Lambeth House. They love being together because they have so many things in common. Of course, their most obvious common interests are Chuck and me! But they also have similar backgrounds, similar life experiences, similar interests, and similar convictions. Both have said that they love the Lord and His church. Their strong common interests have built a strong bond of friendship.

Do you understand your mother's need for friends? Are you helping her develop new peer relationships? Are you encouraging her to maintain contact with longtime friends? Your time and effort will pay off if you assist your mother in relating friend to friend.

Keeping Old Friends

As parents age, they need contact with their special friends more than ever before. Declining health and geographical distance may hinder communication between friends. Also, death takes many older friends. It is in your parent's best interest for them to maintain contact with dear friends. One of the greatest gifts you can give your parents is assistance in seeing or talking with their lifelong friends.

Many of your mother's closest friendships will be with women who raised their children at the same time. Though years have passed, mothers often consider their dearest friends those people who faced similar joys and trials of parenting.

There is history in those relationships. Though time has passed, the close bond of shared experiences will immediately reconnect old friends. It is mutually beneficial for those special friends to keep in touch.

One painful experience in the aftermath of Hurricane Katrina is the scattering of family and friends. People who lived near each other and interacted regularly evacuated to different parts of the country. It was difficult to stay in touch and many missed the closeness of those relationships. As New Orleans rebuilds and resumes life, many people will not return. Families, churches, and neighborhoods will never be the same. Many older people who lost their homes or went to stay with loved ones will have new homes and new neighbors.

Chuck and I are saddened by the knowledge that many of our friends will not return to New Orleans, though we are grateful that our family will be reunited there very soon. Our mothers are saddened by the reality that many of their friends will not be there either. We must work diligently to continue our relationships with dear friends even though we may now live in different places. Change does happen, forcing changes in relationships as well.

Consider how quickly you and a dear friend resume conversation even after a long interval. It is amazing to experience the immediate reconnection. In a matter of moments, the two old friends are talking at a deep, transparent level, sharing personal thoughts and feelings. It seems as if you pick up in midsentence, time has not passed, and you have never been apart. That is a deep relationship with a dear friend.

Chuck and I recently spent a weekend with very special friends. Though we live miles apart and have busy lives, our periodic visits are precious. Since we shared so much for many years as neighbors and colleagues, Karyn and I pick up where we left off. We talk from the heart, sharing blessings and challenges in our lives. I am renewed and refreshed personally by those moments together. I look forward to a future visit and the unique intimacy with a precious friend. Daughters must realize that their mothers also need to spend time with their dear friends.

Mom Kelley keeps in touch with her lifelong friends from Beaumont, Texas, where she lived for more than 40 years. While she has made many friends in Dallas and New Orleans in recent years, most of her closest friends are in Beaumont. They are bonded after all these years because they had babies together, they went to church faithfully together, and they helped each other with their children. Mom Kelley keeps in touch with them regularly through letters, phone calls, and visits. I try to remember the names and some details about her friends, even though I did not know them personally, because she loves talking about her friends. She enthusiastically reports to me the letters and phone calls she receives from friends.

Last year Chuck was invited to preach for Homecoming at his home church in Beaumont. It worked out that I had a speaking engagement that weekend and couldn't go with him. Chuck took his mother back to Beaumont. They enjoyed mother-son time in the car for five hours there and five hours back. On Saturday, Chuck took Mom Kelley back to her favorite beauty shop and then to visit with friends. That night a precious friend hosted a dinner for Mom Kelley and several of their friends. On Sunday, a Homecoming lunch was held after church. She saw so many favorite people. Mom Kelley still talks fondly about her weekend reunion and the best sermon she has ever heard! Of course, her highlight of the weekend was her private time in the car with Chuck, her long-awaited son.

I try to encourage Mom Kelley's communication with friends in various ways. For the last couple of years, I have provided our family members with a list of suggested Christmas gifts for Mom and Papa. I always include note cards, greeting cards, and stamps on Mom Kelley's list. Those gifts are tangible ways for us to encourage Mom Kelley to maintain her contact with old friends. They help her financially by saving that expense, but they also help her socially.

Several years ago, my sister Mitzi gave Mother and me beautiful letter boxes for Christmas. She filled the lovely wooden boxes with assorted stationery and note cards. While the paper products were used up long ago, I still treasure my letter box. Now I store precious notes and cards from dear friends in it. It has become a symbol of love and friendship. I shared my special use of the letter box with my mother, and she began her own collection. We both cherish old friends, and their letters are a precious treasure.

My mother has a dear friend, Janet, who lives in Tennessee. Janet was a faithful friend to Mother as she went through the divorce with my dad. Janet and her husband are moving to Missouri in the near future to be close to their daughter and her family. Mother really wants to go to Janet's home to help her pack and move. My natural tendency is to discourage that because of concern for my mother's health and safety. But I know that Mother will be blessed by the fellowship with her friend. So my sister and I must both agree to support her desire and encourage this special friendship. You must do the same with your mothers—help them maintain contact with their forever friends so their relational needs will be met.

Cultivating New Friends

While older mothers need to stay in touch with lifelong friends, they must also expand their circle of friends. As they move to a new city or lose friends to death, mothers need to meet new people and develop new friendships. There is a tendency toward isolation as parents age and health declines, but you can encourage them to cultivate new friends even in their later stage of life. Though late-in-life friends may not share as much history, they can develop closeness because of similar backgrounds and interests.

Mom Kelley has made an unbelievably positive adjustment to her new life in New Orleans. Since she no longer has the conversational relationship with Papa because of his dementia, she has sought companionship with new friends at Lambeth House and at church. She is intrigued by the culture of New Orleans and has enjoyed getting to know neighbors who are native New Orleanians. She eats lunch in the dining room every day with different friends. Some days my mother joins her, but always Mom Kelley enjoys her "girl talk" at lunch. She has gotten to know new friends at church in her Sunday school class and in other gatherings. In fact, she has developed close friendships with several younger women, a few of my close friends, and even a teenage girl. It is precious to see those friendships blossom.

Chuck has also encouraged his mother's new friendships. He loves to ask her about "the latest gossip from the girls." While she acts embarrassed initially, Mom Kelley quickly begins to fill him in on the details of their table talk. Chuck remembers the names of her sources and often asks specifically about a neighbor or friend. Mom Kelley has remained joyful in her later years not only because of her strong faith in God, but also because she enjoys regular interaction with friends.

I try to encourage new friendships for both of our mothers. At Christmas time, I hosted a party in our home for Mother's Sunday school class and several prospects she was getting to know. Chuck and I invited "the moms" and a new friend at Lambeth House to a Christmas dinner and music program at the seminary. It was my mother's birthday, so we treated the three ladies royally. We arranged for a seminary student to pick them up in a limousine and escort them to the event. My mother and Mom Kelley still talk with glee about their special night, the stretch limo, the handsome young man, and their giggles as they rode in the fancy car.

The first year that the Kelleys were in New Orleans, I hosted a birthday lunch for Mom Kelley in our home. She invited twelve new friends to fill up the dining room table, and we arranged transportation for the group. We enjoyed a delightful time together as we talked around the table. I asked each lady to share about her background and her family. We laughed and cried. That was a significant moment for Mom Kelley to experience with new friends. The occasion also endeared them all to me. I can call each lady by name on the elevator or in the dining room at Lambeth House. You can provide similar opportunities for your mother to make new friends.

A friend shared with me her burden about her mother's isolation. Once a very social, outgoing person, her mother, who was a widow and lived alone, had become very quiet and reclusive. My friend tried to introduce her mother to new people and involve her in senior adult activities, but she was uninterested. Her mother remained isolated and passive. As her health declined, the decision was made for her to move to an assisted living center. Later, my friend reported joyfully that her mother was herself again. She had resumed socializing, had made new friends, and had become busy with many activities. Her health actually improved. She needed friends and interaction with others.

Surely you agree that friendships are very important to women. While all women need special friends, older women have an even greater need for personal friendships. Due to health problems and geographical separation, women can become isolated, lonely, and even depressed. You can facilitate the friendships of your mother. Though you may be stressed by her other needs and the priorities of your own, your support of her friendships will help your mother in significant ways. Encourage your mother to build friendships—keeping in touch with special older friends and cultivating new friends. Her life will be more satisfying and your efforts will be worth the investment.

Mother-Daughter Reflections

1. Who are some of your closest friends and why is their friendship so special to you?

2. Is there an example in the Bible of friendship that speaks meaningfully to you? Why?

3. In what ways do you encourage your mother to maintain contact with old friends?

4. In what ways do you help your mother cultivate new friendships?

5. What can you do in the future to promote your mother's friendships?

Chapter Eleven

Following Biblical Teachings

T he Bible addresses many issues of relevance today. Many biblical principles are meant to guide relationships; among them are teachings about family relationships. Clearly, the Bible instructs parents to love their children and children to love their parents. The Bible includes other truths to guide mothers and daughters in their relationships. We are often urged to seek guidance from many other sources, but Christians should remember to turn first to God's Word for guidance.

God's plan for the parent-child relationship is introduced in the Old Testament and reinforced in the New Testament. The home is a sacred institution to God, and family relationships are integral to all human relationships. In our focus on daughters caring for their mothers in later years, it is helpful to consider key biblical teachings about parents and children. God's Word can and will guide and sustain daughters as they raise their mothers.

Linda, a friend of ours who has a close relationship with the Lord and great confidence in God's Word, relates that her care for her mother is greatly motivated by biblical principles. She told me that her caregiving flows naturally from the commandment to love and honor her parents, even when they disagree. She also believes in the Scriptures that command us "to speak the truth in love," even when it's hard to do, and to wait patiently on the Lord for His will and timing. These are basic biblical principles that give practical guidance in caregiving.

Honor Your Father and Mother

The Bible's plan for families is a straightforward one: Parents are to care for their children until they reach adulthood; children then have a responsibility to care for their aging parents. Care was considered an integral part of "honoring" mothers and fathers, as commanded by God's law. In the Hebrew society, parents and children generally lived together or in close proximity all their lives; they were better able to care for each other because of their close living arrangements. Though today's society often finds parents and their children living far from each other, the biblical mandate still applies. Parents are to care for their children, and children are to honor their parents, all the days of their lives. It is a privilege and responsibility to care for parents.

Moses received the law from God while seeking Him on Mount Sinai. The Ten Commandments were given as a covenant between God and His people. Those basic principles continue to guide human behavior today. Among the commandments like "do not have other gods besides Me" (Exodus 20:3), "remember to dedicate the Sabbath day" (Exodus 20:8), and "do not steal" (Exodus 20:15), God also commanded His children to "honor your father and your mother" (Exodus 20:12). The fifth commandment builds the biblical foundation for adult children to provide for their aging parents. Daughters are instructed by God to honor their mothers always, especially as they enter their later years.

Take a few minutes to examine Exodus 20:12—"Honor your father and your mother so that you may have a long life in the land that the Lord your God is giving you." *Honor* is a verb that means "to show respect for," "to hold in esteem," or "to confer distinction on" (www.dictionary.com). The Bible instructs God's children to "honor the Lord" (Proverbs 3:9), to give Him their utmost love, respect, and esteem. Jesus demonstrated His love and respect for God His Father when the Jews doubted His deity—"I honor My Father" (John 8:49). God, who deserves all honor, is also the source of honor. He gives honor to His children so they can glorify God (2 Peter 1:17). It is also important to remember that in the midst of His death on the cross, Jesus honored and made provision for His mother, Mary (John 19:26–27).

The Hebrew word translated "honor" actually means "treat with respect." Throughout the Old Testament, God's children were commanded to honor others, especially parents. The Lord spoke to Moses in Leviticus 19:3, saying, "Each of you is to respect his mother and father." The Ten Commandments were later reviewed by Moses, who reminded the Israelites to: "Honor your father and your mother, as the Lord your God has commanded you, so that you may live long and so that you may prosper in the land the Lord your God is giving you" (Deuteronomy 5:16). God wanted to make sure that this truth was clear to His people—honor your father and mother.

The commandment to honor is part of a conditional promise by God to His children. *If* you honor your father and mother, *then* your days will be long. Children who love and respect their parents will enjoy the blessings of long life as well as the joy of healthy human relationships. On the other hand, the opposite result will be experienced by children who fail to honor their parents—"cursed is the one who dishonors his father or mother" (Deuteronomy 27:16). The Bible calls children "a heritage from the Lord...a reward" (Psalm 127:3). Children are truly blessings to their parents when they honor them, giving them respect and holding them in esteem.

Dorothy Patterson, my sister-in-law, confirmed that "honor your father and your mother" was the only commandment given with a promise. She recently shared her understanding with me.

> The Lord must have had a reason for setting apart that commandment in such a special way with a promise attached to it, because it was so critically important for us to be obedient. I think again the reason for this goes back to understanding that God has chosen to reveal Himself to us through the family and relationships therein. When we do not practice that honoring of our earthly father and mother, then it makes it that much harder for us to honor our heavenly Father.

The New Testament echoes God's command for children to honor their parents. While speaking to the Pharisees and scribes in Jerusalem, Jesus repeated the command of His Father and gave a harsh punishment: "Honor your father and your mother; and, the one who speaks evil of father or mother must be put to death" (Matthew 15:4). Jesus reminded the Pharisees that giving to God does not to remove the responsibility of caring for your parents. Jesus considered the relationship between children and parents to be sacred. To the rich young ruler, who was selfish with his many earthly possessions, He said: "Honor your father and your mother; and love your neighbor as yourself" (Matthew 19:19). Jesus taught that honor included provision for the material needs of parents.

Paul the apostle taught the followers of Jesus to honor their parents. He gave the Christians in Ephesus guidelines for family relationships: "Children, obey your parents in the Lord, because this is right. Honor your father and mother—which is the first commandment with a promise—that it may go well with you and that you may have long life in the land" (Ephesians 6:1–3). To the Colossians, Paul said: "Children, obey your parents in everything, for this is pleasing in the Lord" (Colossians 3:20). Those who followed Jesus should honor their parents *in everything* and *in all ways*. That honor continues as parents age and is often demonstrated in more tangible ways as the needs of parents increase. As adult children care for their parents, they are obeying the commands of the Lord and pleasing Him. Respectful children will experience personal joy as well as providing blessings for their parents.

While I am certainly not a perfect daughter, I have always sought to honor my parents. Recently, my dad told me I had demonstrated my highest act of honor to him by loving him back to the Lord. When my dad left the Lord and our family, God reminded me that I was to honor my father. While I did not approve of his ungodly lifestyle, I respected his position in my life. Through cards, letters, gifts, and visits, I continually expressed my love for him. He was my father, and I was to honor him, no matter how he acted. God blessed my obedience, and Dad returned to the Lord. Now we are enjoying long life together.

My mother recently reminded me of ways that I honor her. In a thank-you note for our Mother's Day gift, she said: "You honor me most with your godly lives and excellent ministry." I am grateful that she feels honored by my life. I desire to give honor to her spiritually by living a Christlike life. But I also desire to honor her in personal and practical ways. I want to provide her with loving care in her later years as she has provided me with loving care from the day of my birth. It is a greater privilege than it is a responsibility to honor parents.

A friend named Mary affirmed the biblical command to honor parents. She explained that the biblical principle applies across the life span. From childhood through adulthood, a child is to honor her father and mother. I agree with Mary that "there is no time limit on honoring." Christians must obey God's command in relationship with their parents and teach this truth to their children.

Build a Godly Heritage

The Bible also challenges Christians to leave a godly legacy, to pass along a heritage of faith to their families and the generations to follow. The faith lived out in the lives of parents is to be handed down from generation to generation. Proverbs speaks often about the relationship between parent and child, as well as the importance of sharing a spiritual legacy.

Proverbs 1:8—"Listen, my son, to your father's instruction, and don't reject your mother's teaching."

Proverbs 4:1—"Listen, my sons, to a father's discipline, and pay attention so that you may gain understanding."

Proverbs 15:20—"A wise son brings joy to his father, but a foolish one despises his mother."

Proverbs 22:6—"Teach a youth about the way he should go; even when he is old he will not depart from it."

Proverbs 23:25—"Let your father and mother have joy, and let her who gave birth to you rejoice."

(See also Proverbs 6:20; 13:1; 15:5; 19:26; 28:24; 29:3; 30:11, 17.)

It is clear throughout the Book of Proverbs that both fathers and mothers are expected to raise their children in the Lord. Both sons and daughters are to honor their parents, obey their biblical instructions, follow their godly examples, and heed their wise counsel. Proverbs 23:22 gives direct instruction for children: "Listen to your father who gave you life, and don't despise your mother when she is old." Children should continue to love and honor their parents, not neglecting them in their twilight years.

My friend Debbie recalls the Old Testament example of Naomi when she thinks of her mother. The widow Naomi passed along a legacy of faith to her daughter-in-law Ruth. As a young widow, Debbie's mother "moved forward, even in the midst of tragedy, without bitterness." She is aware of God's blessings and passes along that legacy of hope to her children and grandchildren. Debbie has concluded that her mother's life is a wonderful example of faith and a pattern for her to pass along to her own children.

The New Testament also teaches about the spiritual legacy passed from parent to child. Jesus received a legacy of faith from Mary and Joseph. They took Him to the temple at the appropriate times in His development. His adult ministry reflected a childhood of Scripture memory and meditation (Matthew 4). Paul commented on his own religious heritage and Timothy was reminded by Paul of his godly training in the home. In 2 Timothy, Paul gratefully recalled young Timothy's spiritual heritage:

> I constantly remember you in my prayers night and day…recalling your sincere faith that first lived in your grandmother Lois, then in your mother Eunice, and that I am convinced is in you also. Therefore, I remind you to keep ablaze the gift of God that is in you.
> —2 Timothy 1:3–6

The faith of Timothy's grandmother Lois was passed along to his mother Eunice, and then to him. Timothy had the responsibility of continuing his family's legacy of faith.

Carole Lewis and her granddaughter Cara Symank pay tribute to their own mothers in *The Mother-Daughter Legacy*. Each daughter shares legacies left by their mothers that they treasure and seek to emulate. They suggest these mother-daughter legacies that can be passed along from one generation to the next:

1. **The legacy of nurture:** A mother cares for the physical, emotional, and spiritual needs of her children.
2. **The legacy of family:** A mother gathers the ones she loves around her and keeps them connected together.
3. **The legacy of example:** A mother's character is reflected in her daily life.
4. **The legacy of giving:** A mother gives totally of herself, her time, and her possessions.
5. **The legacy of acceptance:** A mother loves her children unconditionally and accepts them as they are.

A mother who leaves these legacies is a blessing, but a mother who loves Jesus and lives a Christlike life leaves an even greater legacy—a legacy of faith.

Our friend Lisa has been blessed by the godly legacy of her parents. She appreciates the lessons her mother has taught her: gentle strength through her weakness, the gift of giving, and the gift of hospitality, which is another lost art today. Lisa is also grateful for her father's godly example. He has taught her "to always, always believe in God, in self, and in mankind." Lisa is thankful for the strength, unconditional love, and confidence that her father has passed along to her. She now has the opportunity to pass this legacy of faith along to her own son.

As the years pass, the daughter who has received from her mother these gifts of legacy begins to give them to her mother in return. It is the daughter who nurtures the mother in her later years, keeps the family connected, lives out Christian character, gives generously of time and resources, and accepts her mother's limitations. As the daughter receives a godly legacy from her mother, she is able to pass the legacy on to her daughter and to others. The special bond between mother and daughter sustains them throughout their lives and is passed along to the next generation. What a mother gives to others she will receive in return later in life.

I am very grateful for my family legacy. I have received a legacy of faith from my grandmothers and mother. My mother has instilled in me by word and example a passionate love for the Lord, a profound respect for His Word, a complete devotion to His church, sacrificial giving to His kingdom, gracious hospitality to His children, and unselfish ministry to those in need. I have received a tremendous legacy of faith from my godly mother. It is now my turn to live out my faith and pass it on to the next generation. While I do not have children of my own in whom to pour this legacy, God has placed me in positions of leadership, giving me many opportunities to leave lasting legacies through students and other women who are my spiritual daughters. God teaches His children to honor their fathers and mothers as well as leave legacies of faith.

Teach the Young to Love Their Elders

The Bible also instructs Christians to love their elders. "The elders of Israel" are mentioned throughout the Old Testament, suggesting the high esteem the ancient world gave older people. Age alone deserved great respect. The patriarchs gave honor to their forefathers and received honor from their children. Joseph and his brothers shared a deep love for their father. Despite the hate and betrayal between the brothers, each of them continued to love and respect Jacob. Joseph mourned his father's death and obeyed his deathbed request to forgive the brothers for their treachery. Joseph understood what they intended for evil, God made for good (Genesis 50:20). He honored his father, forgave his brothers, and cared for his family. (See Joseph's story in Genesis 36–50.) Ruth demonstrated her love and devotion to her mother-in-law, Naomi, as she followed Naomi's God, accompanied her back to Bethlehem, and provided for her needs (Ruth 1–4).

The New Testament also encourages Christians to love their elders. Jesus respected His elders, though He did not always practice their religious rituals (Matthew 15:1–9; Mark 7:1–23). He provided salvation by faith while esteeming those older than Himself who needed His salvation. He taught His followers to care for the widows and elderly. And on the cross, Jesus insured that His own mother would be cared for after His death: "He said to the disciple, 'Here is your mother.'

From that hour the disciple took her into his home" (John 19:27). Even in His agony, Jesus was concerned about the future welfare of His mother. As the eldest son, Jesus took the responsibility of providing for John to be His mother's protector and provider. What an example for children to respect their elders and care for their mothers!

Our society today seems to have lost its profound respect for the elderly. In general, children are not taught to respect authority. People of position or advanced age may be shunned or neglected. The Bible convicts Christians today to love, honor, and respect their elders! Christians would do well to follow the biblical teachings of Paul. In 1 Timothy 5, Paul gives instructions for ministry, beginning with ministry to older people: "Do not rebuke an older man, but exhort him as a father, younger men as brothers, older women as mothers, and with all propriety, the younger women as sisters" (1 Timothy 5:1–2). Followers of Christ are to respect people who are older as they would their fathers or their mothers. Love and honor are due those in their later years. Care and provision are outward expressions of love and honor.

In the following verses of 1 Timothy 5, Paul specifically addresses care of widows, older women who have lost their husbands ("genuinely widows," verse 3). He gave specific responsibility first to any offspring: "If any widow has children or grandchildren, they should learn to practice their religion toward their own family first and to repay their parents, for this pleases God" (1 Timothy 5:4). Later, Paul gives a warning to those children who don't care for their parents: "If anyone does not provide for his own relatives, and especially for his household, he has denied the faith and is worse than an unbeliever" (1 Timothy 5:8). If widows do not have children, they are to be cared for by the church. God's plan provides for the widows through their own children or other believers.

Paul concludes his instructions for ministry in 1 Timothy 5 with a charge to honor elders. In this passage, he specifically addresses older leaders—elders (bishops or pastors). The position of leadership in the church and the age of the leader are due honor. If the performance of an elder is questioned, accusations must be substantiated. Age and position should be revered. Criticism of seniors cannot be taken lightly. The Scripture is clear: the young are to love their elders and provide for them.

A friend named Margaret was reminded by her son that children should remember their elders. He said to his mother, "Don't forget Nonnie. She has done so much for us. And God tells us to respect our elders." Her son's biblical advice has encouraged Margaret as she cares for her 94-year-old mother, who is in the advanced stages of Alzheimer's disease. God does command us to love and respect our elders. By word and example, we can teach our children to respect us, their elders.

Christians today should love and care for their elders. The seniors of our society have many needs. The body of Christ, following His plan, can help them financially and spiritually. As Christians minister to the elderly, the young people in the church see the command of God lived out in lives. The younger generations will better understand why to honor and how to care for their elders if Christians today care for their parents and other elders.

My mother is involved in many ministries of our church. However, one of her most significant contributions is to the Heritage Committee. She and other church members are compiling biographies of life deacons in our church and building a lasting legacy for future leaders. Young deacons have been asked to interview the older deacons, then summaries are written about their lives and ministries. Special relationships are being developed between the juniors and seniors as they learn about the past. While it is a very time-consuming task, the written record will provide a permanent legacy of faithfulness.

Years ago, Mom Kelley began writing her story. She humbly denies living an important life, but she wants her children and grandchildren to remember their family heritage. Chapter by chapter, she is building the legacy that will be passed along to future generations. Her weekly letter to the family further develops the legacy. What a gift to our family! All families would be enriched by a written family history.

Daughters obey God's Word as they care for their mothers. Care includes respecting their feelings, listening to their wishes, considering their opinions, sacrificing to meet their needs, and appreciating their investment of time and energy in parenting. It is never too early to develop a loving relationship between mother and daughter. In fact, those daughters who have always had a close, comfortable relationship with their mothers will have a stronger relationship in later years. When the daughter becomes the mother, the bond of love will endure through the years of struggles. The care needed by an aging mother will not be so much a burden as a blessing!

Mother-Daughter Reflections

1. Which specific biblical teachings about parents and children encourage you to care for your parents in their later years?

2. In what practical ways do you honor your father and mother?

3. In what practical ways are you continuing a godly heritage?

4. In what ways are you teaching the young to love their elders?

5. How has God blessed you for the love and care you give to your parents? In what ways?

Chapter Twelve

Heeding Practical Advice

F ormer First Lady Rosalynn Carter has said, "there are only four kinds of people in the world: those who have been caregivers, those who are, those who will be, and those who will need care." Almost everyone will be a caregiver at some time, and most of us will need caregiving ourselves. In the cycle of life, the time comes when people are unable to care for themselves and need to be cared for by others.

Caregiving can be a tremendous challenge or a tremendous blessing. The work of caregiving is all consuming and can take a great toll from the caregiver. However, there are many rewards for loving service.

Many resources are available to assist and support caregivers. Heeding practical advice can also help the caregiver enjoy the blessings of caregiving. This chapter will discuss six specific suggestions for caregivers.

Set Limits

The needs of every senior adult are different and the circumstances of every caregiver are different. As a result, it is essential to understand the needs of all people involved and set personal limits. While all relationships need boundaries in order to be healthy, the relationship between an older person and a caregiver, an aging mother and caregiving daughter, will need well-defined boundaries because of increasing needs. Everyone involved benefits when realistic limits are set.

Throughout our marriage, my husband Chuck has calmed my anxieties with the truthful saying, "All you can do is all you can do, and all you can do is enough." When I am stressed by my many responsibilities or I am overwhelmed by the things that face me, Chuck reminds me of this truth. While it is hard for many obsessive-compulsive women like me to accept our limitations, in reality, the things that must get done do get done. In many ways, this practical principle helps me establish some personal boundaries.

When it comes to setting limits as a caregiver, you should honestly answer these questions:

1. What *must* be done?
2. When *must* it be done?
3. Can *anyone else* do it?
4. Can *Mother* do it herself?
5. What *can* I do?

As you answer these questions, you can clarify the degree of urgency with your mother and establish some priorities for yourself. You can also discuss your other responsibilities while you express your concern about her needs.

As you set limits, you must learn how to separate needs from wants. There is a significant difference between the real needs of your parent (food, clothing, shelter, medical care) and their personal desires (longer visits with you, shopping excursions, better health). Realistically, you should focus on meeting her real needs. While it would be nice to grant some wishes, they are not essential for life and can be granted when possible.

Learn to say "no." It is hard to refuse a request, especially from an aging parent. However, sometimes you must say no and sometimes no is best. Try to say no gently. You can decline a request in a loving, caring manner. A friend of mine likes to say, "Learn to say no with your teeth showing." In other words, smile as you say no.

It may help you to plan your responses before you are forced to set limits. As you encounter unnecessary requests, you can confidently yet lovingly respond. I have several frequent replies to my mothers when my time is short and their needs do not seem urgent. "Let me call you back later when there is more time to talk." "I am going to the drug store on Monday if you need anything." "I'll be in your neighborhood tomorrow if you would like for me to stop by." With these comments, I communicate my love and concern, but I also control my time.

Setting limits helps a caregiver manage her own responsibilities and control her feelings of guilt. Guilt is a typical emotion for women and is the driving force behind many actions. Daughters caring for their aging mothers must resist feelings of guilt if they are unable to grant all of their mothers' wishes. Guilt is heavy baggage to carry, causing hurt to the parent and child alike. Setting realistic limits ahead of time will reduce those feelings of guilt.

Develop Systems

To survive, the caregiver's life must be systemized. You will feel more productive if you develop a process for every area of life. Organizing time and arranging activities in an orderly manner will save time, promote efficiency, and simplify life. Systems will help anticipate needs and eliminate anxieties. Even if you are not organized by nature, a caregiver must develop systems in order to maximize service and minimize stress.

Specific systems are beneficial because they bring order to an older person's daily life and promote security through routine. Observe the regular activities of your loved one, then help her develop systems for the future.

Time Management. Everyone benefits from a daily schedule, but senior adults need one. Help your mother establish a schedule of daily activities and follow it except in emergencies and during special times of the year. A typical daily schedule should include a time for

- waking up
- bathing
- dressing
- eating breakfast
- toileting
- exercising
- eating lunch
- having social interaction
- eating dinner
- getting ready for bed
- other personal activities

There is security in sameness as well as excitement in newness. Special activities during holidays or family visits will be appreciated more when they are a departure from the typical routine.

Chuck's mother loves her morning routine. After waking up, Mom Kelley begins her day with prayer time, then gets dressed and eats breakfast. She eats the same breakfast every day. Then she reads her paper and watches a favorite television program. When her daughters visit, they know not to interfere with her morning routine. They arrive at lunch and enjoy an afternoon visit. Mom Kelley loves her regular routine, but occasionally enjoys departure from the same schedule. In one of her weekly letters, Mom Kelley recalled a special afternoon with her sweetheart:

> Yesterday, I had arranged for Dad to have a pedicure at the first floor beauty shop. After that, I took him up to our apartment to stay until about 4:30. We had a good "Coke party" with three cookies for him. He has not been drinking the Coke every day, but he did yesterday. I took him back to get ready for his dinner. I was glad that it all worked out well, and I think he enjoyed it. He usually seems to do better if he stays in his familiar surroundings, but it was nice to see him enjoy the change of scenery.

It is precious to see God bless the time the Kelleys have together.

Meal Management. It is important for seniors to eat a healthy diet. Proper nutrition promotes good health and sustains energy. Talk with your mother about her daily food intake. Assist her in following medical diets. Help her make decisions about meal management, considering
- favorite foods
- simple menus
- easy-to-make recipes
- weekly meal planning
- grocery list

- prepared foods
- meals out per week

You can help your mother set limits for her diet to promote good health and control unnecessary demands on your time.

Chuck takes meal planning seriously. He carefully considers his mother's food preferences as well as her need to get out. At least once a week, we try to take her out to eat. Of course, the Texas Kelleys must have Mexican food regularly, so we often enjoy an outing to a Mexican restaurant. In talking about meals, we can also verify that Mom Kelley is eating well and that she has the groceries she needs at home.

Medical Management. There will be a greater need for a system of health care management as your mother ages. She will need a daily schedule of medicines and a plan for renewing prescriptions. Regular medical checkups need to be arranged. Plastic daily medicine boxes and calendars with marked prescription refill dates can help reduce emergencies. A routine for doctor's visits and a current medical history insure good health care. Caregivers benefit from learning some basic nursing skills and securing appropriate home health services. Recognize that illnesses will be contracted and you cannot prevent death. There are limits to health care.

Chuck's sister Charlene is a nurse. She has helped the Kelley family be health conscious. Because of her training, she monitors their medical condition and informs us if medical problems seem apparent. Charlene made these suggestions about medical management for parents: "Keep an accurate medical history, schedule regular checkups, learn their desires about medical treatment, ask the doctor about their medications, recognize physical changes, and report reactions to medications." Caregivers must help their loved ones manage their medical care.

Financial Management. Your mother will benefit from a system of financial management. If your loved one doesn't have a professional financial planner, you can help with business affairs by securing one. Since financial investments and legal guidelines are complicated, professional expertise is helpful. Encourage your mother to use direct deposits for pension checks and regular income. Establish a method for depositing checks received. Assist as needed in writing checks and balancing monthly bank statements. Help your mother develop a realistic budget and live within it. However, understand that your mother may spend her money in ways you don't approve. Until she is unable, your mother should control her own purse strings. You should only get involved when her decisions lead to serious financial risks. I am so grateful that both of our mothers have organized systems for management of their financial affairs.

Relationship Management. Since your mother needs interaction with others, you must help her keep in touch. Install a simple portable telephone for ease in communication. Preset important phone numbers for automatic dial or compile a list of numbers in an address book or on a posted reference sheet. Keep an updated address list as well as stationery, envelopes, return labels, and stamps. Provide a "Special Dates" book to remember birthday and anniversaries. Purchase a supply of greeting cards and assist in securing gifts as needed. Arrange for visits with family members and friends. While you cannot *make* your mother happy or *force* her to get along with other people, you can encourage her to maintain personal relationships.

Follow Routines

Systems are helpful to the caregiver and the care receiver. In addition to organizational processes, routines and schedules are beneficial to aging parent and caring child. There is security in routines and confidence in care. Consider typical activities and schedule them regularly.

When weddings or other major events are planned, specific schedules are followed in order to manage the many details. Tasks are listed according to the time frame required for planning. Checklists include things to be done a year, a month, a week, or a day ahead. Because the responsibilities of a caregiver include a multitude of details, it is helpful to develop a regular schedule and follow a regimented routine. Consider the routine below, then customize one for yourself.

Daily
- Call by phone for update.
- Make sure that medicines are taken.
- Verify three meals are eaten.
- Encourage social interaction.
- Ensure personal hygiene.
- Respond to any emergencies.

Weekly
- Visit personally or arrange for a visit from family or friend.
- Make drugstore purchases.
- Go out to eat if possible.
- Schedule beauty shop appointment if desired.
- Run other errands if needed.
- Encourage regular exercise.
- Promote group interaction.
- Coordinate an outside trip if possible.

Monthly
- Schedule doctor's appointments as recommended.
- Renew prescriptions as required.

- Assist with paying bills and balancing checkbook if needed.
- Check home for safety and repairs.

Annually
- Assist with preparation of tax returns.
- Meet with financial planner to discuss budget and investments.
- Take a trip to visit relatives or friends if possible.
- Schedule complete annual physical.

There is another positive benefit to routines. While they ensure the needs of older loved ones are met and they help the caregiver control time, routines are also vehicles for involving others in the caregiving process. Family members who live out of town can make daily phone calls, schedule weekly visits, assist with monthly reminders, and participate in annual visits.

While I regularly provide for the needs of the Kelleys, their daughters and grandchildren are actively involved in their lives even from a distance. The daughters call daily, write often, and visit regularly. Grandchildren also keep in touch and send pictures of the great grandchildren. One of the Kelleys' granddaughters has been very faithful in taking them out to eat, to the movies, and even on short trips whenever possible. Everyone in the family can be a part of the parents' routine.

Understand a Parent's Perspective
Throughout the process of caregiving it is important to try to understand your parent's perspective. Everyone deserves respect and appreciation. Your parent deserves love and devotion. So even when your own life is overwhelming and your personal bias is strong, it is helpful to think from the parent's

perspective. Try to be sensitive to your aging parent's needs, desires, and feelings.

Older adults are usually concerned about their independence and economic stability. Having experienced the Great Depression, senior adults are more worried about their future livelihood than the younger generations. They are not used to being dependent upon others and they don't want to be a burden to their children. Try to minimize your own efforts and don't complain about inconveniences in caring for their needs. Understand how hard it is for your parents to ask for help and anticipate their needs when possible.

Older adults may have different values than you, and they may make different choices. Every personality is different and lifestyles may vary, so priorities may not be the same. Don't get upset with your parents when they do something you would not do. Allow them to make personal decisions as long as possible. Different is not good or bad, right or wrong—it is simply different. Give your parents the same room to make their own decisions as they gave you as you were growing up.

Even when you become the caregiver, your parents are still your parents. Always honor your parents. Be grateful for their provision and nurture early in your life. Recognize their influence and guidance. Acknowledge their unconditional love and unselfish support. As you care for them, seek to return those personal investments. Never look down on them and avoid being condescending. Even in their declining years, your parents are of great worth and value in God's eyes. So treat them with honor and respect.

One of the best ways to understand your parents' perspective is to keep the chain of communication open. Talk about feelings and desires. Ask questions and listen carefully to comments. It is never too early to start learning about your parents and understanding them.

My husband, Chuck, is very perceptive. He has an uncanny ability to understand the personalities of other people and recognize their interests. He likes to call himself a "Rhonda scholar" because he knows me so well. Chuck also knows his mother better than anyone does. He seems to understand her better than she understands herself. It is obvious in little ways. He loves to buy her books, and he always knows what she likes to read. Though he is busy, Chuck takes time to call his mother after her Astros win a baseball game or when the news headlines are of interest to her. I also try to understand the perspectives of Mom Kelley and my mother. It takes time and effort, but it builds a stronger relationship.

I made a personal observation in a previous chapter: it seems that a daughter is sometimes better able to understand her mother-in-law's perspective than her own mother's perspective. There seems to be a tendency for a daughter to judge her mother and be less tolerant, whereas a daughter-in-law may listen and observe more patiently. Daughters tend to tell their mothers what to do. Daughters-in-law are generally hesitant to give direction. I see that difference personally. While Chuck's four sisters seem to give instructions to their mother, I tend to listen to my mother-in-law and implement her desires. However, I find myself telling my own mother what to do. Daughters must try to understand and adapt to their mothers' perspectives.

Care for the Caregiver

It is difficult but essential for the caregiver to care for herself. Women are often guilty of sacrificing their own needs and risking their own health to care for others. Mothers unselfishly give of themselves to their children, denying themselves. Daughters may also care for their aging mothers to their own personal detriment. It is true that a caregiver cannot give if she is not cared for herself. My friend Cyndi shares this conviction. She adds, "Don't feel guilty when you need time away from caregiving. Time away will help you and your loved one. It will help you to be patient with them and yourself." How true!

As you juggle your many responsibilities, don't forget yourself. You need to be healthy—physically, mentally, and spiritually. So find time for yourself and find ways to strengthen yourself. Don't let love, loyalty, or guilt drive you to care for your mother at the cost of your own health or the happiness of your family.

In recent article in *Newsweek* (June 21, 2004), "The Keys to Caregiving," author Julie Scelfo suggested that caregivers follow these guidelines to avoid burnout:

- Ask for help.
- Get support.
- Change your habits.
- Take a break.

Many family members or friends would love to assist you with caregiving responsibilities. Their help will be good for all of you, so ask for specific assistance. Many support services are available to the elderly and to caregivers. Find them in your own community or online. (See the chapter on resources and the list at the back of this book for additional help.) Make adjustments in your own behavior and lifestyle to limit frustration and reduce stress. Also, stop and rest. Take a nap or read a book every day to renew yourself and prepare for future caregiving.

The topic of caregiving is often in the press today. Even the publishing world is responding with specialized magazines—*Today's Caregiver, Caring Today,* and *Vantage.* These publications focus solely on the subject, whereas other periodicals may have a different focus but include articles about caregiving. Recent features have addressed how to involve family members, relaxation techniques, caregiving from afar, and stories from the trenches. It is obvious that caregivers need care too.

A recent article in *Cooking Light* (September 2005), "Care for the Caregiver" by Susan Colon, reinforces the prevalence of helpful resources and support programs. In addition, it suggested specific ways for caregivers to take care of themselves:

- **Start a journal:** Record your feelings and experiences.
- **Eat a healthy diet:** Avoid saturated fats and indulge in fruits, vegetables, and whole grains.
- **Schedule exercise:** Maintain regular exercise to reduce stress and improve health.
- **Try to get enough sleep:** Attempt to sleep 7 to 8 hours each night.
- **Stay in touch with friends:** Continue social interaction and stay connected with special people.

Though effort is involved to care for yourself, the benefits are experienced when caregivers give themselves some tender loving care (TLC). To be an effective caregiver, you must be cared for yourself.

Remember the Blessings

It is very easy to get so caught up with and overwhelmed by the work of caregiving that you forget the worth of caregiving. Days are filled with errands and emergencies. Time is pressured by the needs of children and parents. The big picture is clouded by the many details. Don't let caregiving be a burden. Think of it as a blessing. Always recall the joys of time together and the memories of the past. Try not to let the difficult days drown out the blessings of the Lord.

Our friend Marion agrees that caring for parents is a blessing. In fact, she suggests that the most profound blessing is the role reversal. "For so many years, children have been on the receiving end of the parents' giving. In later life, the situation is reversed. Children are called to be the givers and parents the receivers." What a blessing!

A recent cartoon strip in *For Better or for Worse* reminded me of the importance of a positive attitude and a focus on life's little blessings. An elderly couple was out for a walk. The older man was using a walker and was forced to look down to ensure his safety. But he saw the benefits of his limitation: "Looking down has its good points. I pay more attention to the flowers now. I see moss growing through the sidewalk. And sometimes there's a name or a hand print left in the cement. Every day there's a treasure to find if you know where to look." His wife understood what he meant. The elderly man focused on the blessings, not the burdens of his life. We can learn from him to accentuate the positive and eliminate the negative.

When you feel overwhelmed by the demands of caregiving, recall the sacrifices your mother made for you as a child. When you are tired from your caregiving duties, remember the unconditional love of your mother. When your mother's needs seem insurmountable, realize the blessings of caring for your loved one. God will empower you to support your aging mother, so you should recognize the blessings and give glory to Him.

Happiness

A story entitled "Happiness" by an unknown author was recently circulated on the Internet. The 92-year-old lady in the story teaches by her actions and attitudes that happiness is a choice. People choose each day to be happy and to feel blessed. As you read the story, make a commitment to remember the blessings of caregiving.

The 92-year-old, well-poised and proud lady, who is fully dressed each morning by eight o'clock, with her hair fashionably coifed and makeup perfectly applied, even though she is legally blind, moved to a nursing home today. Her husband of 70 years recently passed away, making the move necessary.

After many hours of waiting patiently in the lobby of the nursing home, she smiled sweetly when told her room was ready.

As she maneuvered her walker to the elevator, I provided a visual description of her tiny room, including the eyelet sheets that had been hung on her window. "I love it," she stated with the enthusiasm of an eight-year-old having just been presented with a new puppy.

"Mrs. Jones, you haven't seen the room…just wait."

"That doesn't have anything to do with it," she replied. "Happiness is something you decide on ahead of time. Whether I like my room or not doesn't depend on how the furniture is arranged…it's how I arrange my mind.

"I already decided to love it. It's a decision I make every morning when I wake up. I have a choice: I can spend the day in bed recounting the difficulty I have with the parts of my body that no longer work, or get out of bed and be thankful for the ones that do. Each day is a gift, and as long as my eyes are open I'll focus on the new day and all the happy memories I've stored away just for this time in my life.

"Old age is like a bank account: you withdraw from what you've put in. So, my advice to you would be to deposit a lot of happiness in the bank account of memories.

"Thank you for your part in filling my memory bank. I am still depositing."

What words of wisdom about remembering the blessings of life! If a 92-year-old can focus on the blessings, you can too.

Much practical advice is available to caregivers today. This chapter summarized a few recommendations. Loving caregivers should set some realistic limits, develop some specific systems, follow regular routines, and understand their parents' perspectives. Some personal care for the caregiver is essential, too. When such recommendations are followed, the blessings of caregiving can surpass the challenges.

Mother-Daughter Reflections

1. What limits do you need to set for your caregiving?

2. What systems and schedules have you and your mother developed to promote efficiency?

3. What is your mother's perspective about her condition and her caregiving needs?

4. What are the blessings you experience in caregiving?

5. What caregiving advice would you share with others who are caring for their parents?

Chapter Thirteen

Involving Church Support

C hristians are strengthened by the presence of the Holy Spirit and guided by the principles of Scripture at all times, especially when aging or caregiving. In addition, Christians are supported by God's children, who provide prayer and ministry in times of need. The body of Christ, the church, is a biblical source of help and encouragement. Older Christians are blessed as they continue to worship and serve. Caregivers can receive training, support, and fellowship as members of a body of believers.

Many churches have active ministries with senior adults. Effective ministries are *with* senior adults, not *to* senior adults. In other words, staff members and church leaders should not provide a ministry *for* older members. Instead, the leadership must work *with* the seniors to meet their needs and involve them in service. Senior adult ministry is a participatory program, not a spectator sport. Older adults must stay active in the Lord's work. Today that is a more realistic goal than ever before because seniors are living longer and staying healthier.

Churches offer a wide range of programs and ministries for senior adults. The scope is determined by the needs of the members, the resources of the church, and the commitment of the staff. While each ministry will vary, it is important for the senior adults to have a balanced program. Ongoing ministries and special opportunities should offer spiritual enrichment, learning experiences, regular socialization, service opportunities, and personal services. In this chapter, we will explore five ministries for senior adults in the church. Balanced senior adult ministries should encourage spiritual growth as well as provide educational seminars, small groups, home visitation, and meaningful ministry.

Spiritual Growth

All Christians are to grow in faith. While senior adults may have known the Lord for many years, they don't know all they need to know about Him. Continued spiritual growth is essential. More than ever in their lives, seniors who are retired and have fewer demands on their time can devote themselves to prayer, study of God's Word, and service through His church. Senior adults must not be satisfied to count on their past walk with the Lord, but they must cultivate an even closer relationship with Him in their later years.

Faith can grow stronger even when health fades and abilities diminish. Older Christians learn total dependence upon the Lord. The more helpless they become, the more trust in the Lord is required. Christians in their later years can leave a godly legacy because of their unfailing faith in God.

Caregivers can encourage the spiritual growth of their loved ones. Visits can include shared prayer times and Bible study. Words of witness can promote active sharing of personal testimonies. Inspirational books and prayer journals can be given to those seniors still able to read and comprehend. Excitement about spiritual growth is contagious, and evidence of a close relationship with the Lord is inspiring.

Prayer is a spiritual discipline that can be practiced throughout the last years of life. Conversation with God about personal needs and the needs of others can be voiced aloud or silently. There is power and hope in prayer. The faithful prayer life of an older Christian strengthens others as well as themselves. Many of the greatest prayer warriors are in their later years. Their prayer life can be deep and long, unencumbered by busy schedules and work demands. However, like all Christians, older adults must discipline themselves to pray.

As mentioned previously, Mom Kelley is a faithful prayer warrior. She prays passionately and purposefully every morning for about two hours. She prays by name for each member of the family, mentioning their particular needs. She also prays for friends and for shared requests. Last year, I asked her to pray for ten ladies who requested prayer at our annual Ladies' Afternoon Tea. Mom Kelley immediately agreed to be a part of our prayer follow-up team. She continues to pray specifically for each lady a year after the event. Occasionally she asks me about one of the ladies so she can know if God has answered her prayers. What an example of the discipline of prayer!

Bible study is another important spiritual discipline that can be practiced by many senior adults. Personal study of God's Word can reveal His plan and provision for His children. Many Bible study resources are produced to assist Christians in understanding the Scripture. Bible study groups can meet frequently to share what God has taught individual members. Older Christians can increase, as Jesus did, "in wisdom…and in favor with God and with people" (Luke 2:52).

Both of my mothers are active students of God's Word. They attend Sunday school regularly and always study their lessons. Over the years, they have learned much about Scripture. Each of them is also involved in a small group Bible study. Mom Kelley enjoys a weekly group at Lambeth House, while my mother attends a weekly Bible study sponsored by the women's ministry at our church. It is an encouragement to me and others to hear them quote Scriptures or discuss spiritual truths learned in their recent study of God's Word.

Evangelism is another spiritual discipline to be continued in later years. Senior adults can and should talk freely about the Lord and His work in their lives. A personal testimony of faith is a powerful tool of evangelism. Older Christians who reflect the joy of the Lord and share His blessings proclaim a more profound message than a hundred sermons. Senior adults need to be equipped to share the gospel and encouraged to speak the truth.

Papa Kelley has always been a radiant witness. I have so many fond memories of Papa being on elevators and turning around to speak a word of encouragement to the occupants—"It's a beautiful day in the Lord" or "Smile, God loves you." What a testimony of the joy of the Lord! Since moving to Lambeth House, Papa and Mom Kelley have faithfully attended the Sunday afternoon chapel services, even though some services that were not of their preferred denomination have been less than inspiring to them. They carry their Bibles, and Papa often asks someone in passing, "Have you read the Good Book today?" I love to hear him quote Scripture and sing hymns. They are both such vibrant witnesses for the Lord.

A Christian's call to faith is lifelong. As Christians age, they must renew their commitment to spiritual growth. Older Christians need more commitment, not less; more creativity, not less; more concentration, not less. Devoted senior adults can strengthen their own lives spiritually and stimulate the growth of the church.

Educational Seminars

Even in the later years, there is much knowledge to be acquired and many lessons to be learned. In fact, age cannot be used as an excuse to stop education. Experts in aging have concluded that the ability to learn does not decline over the years; only the rate or speed of learning decreases with age. While the aging process does impair cognitive function, most senior adults can continue learning in their twilight years. Geriatric research and personal experience have verified the reality of intellectual growth in senior adults.

Margaret Burks got a standing ovation when she earned her master's degree from New Orleans Baptist Theological Seminary several years ago. It was a great accomplishment, especially since she was 86 years of age. After graduation, the retired accountant spent two years on the mission field in Tanzania. She still plans to earn a PhD in psychology in the future. What a testimony of the learning potential in an older adult.

Educational opportunities are often offered to senior adults in their retirement centers, in community centers, in hospitals, and in churches. Information should be provided about health concerns, financial management, and personal enrichment. Older people can increase knowledge about technology and modern advances while they are allaying their fears about the future. Many seniors take continuing education courses in computers to learn how to communicate with family members by email and gain information on the Internet. They purchase cell phones to keep in touch with loved ones. Some even learn to text message grandchildren. DVDs, iPods, and personal digital assistants may help seniors enjoy life. Technology doesn't have to be scary to senior adults. It can help them personally and in relationships with others if they are carefully taught the use. Training is essential and stimulates the mind.

Our family had a delightful experience during the Thanksgiving holidays when my 20-year-old nephew tried to teach my mother how to text message on her cell phone. While Mother has become quite proficient with her cell phone, she had never attempted to text message. Dent patiently demonstrated to his Mimi how to send a typed-out message. When the training session ended, Mother confidently typed a message to her grandson. She hit send and Dent's phone rang. He read her brief message and began to laugh. Mother had typed "Hekko" instead of "Hello." We all laughed and throughout the weekend we greeted each other with a loud, loving, "Hekko!" Even though we teased her, I was proud that Mother was not threatened by technology. In fact, she loves to text message her grandkids.

Churches can promote learning among senior adults by providing educational seminars. Conferences relevant to specific needs and concerns of older people can be organized. Specific topics may include community issues, current events, financial management, legal matters, medical concerns, health and wellness, and safety measures. Brief one- or two-hour daytime sessions that offer printed information and that allow time for discussion seem most helpful to seniors.

In addition, for senior adult classes, churches should enlist teachers who understand the unique needs and learning styles of senior adults. Howard McClusky identified five need categories of persons in the later years (*Learning for Aging*). With each of the five specified needs, he provided a corresponding question to be answered if older adults are to learn:

- **Coping** needs: How do we cope with the loss of job, friends, spouse, money, and/or influence?
- **Expressive** needs: How do we help people share themselves, their gifts and resources, with others?
- **Contributive** needs: How do we help individuals give and feel needed?
- **Influence** needs: How can we help everyone make some impact on society?
- **Transcendence** needs: How do we help people find meaningful life and death?

Older adults will continue growing and learning if caregivers and churches help meet their needs and provide appropriate training. Teachers of senior adults must understand their needs and respond to their learning styles. Because later life bombards seniors with serious life-altering change, they often seem to resist change that is not absolutely essential. However, seniors will change if the reasoning is explained and the process is gradual. The church must keep seniors in mind as change is proposed.

Remember to consider the anxieties seniors feel when faced with new information. Simple, clear instructions should be repeated patiently. Encouragement and assistance are helpful. A relaxed, informal setting may be less threatening. Teaching methods should be varied: include discussion, media presentations, storytelling, demonstrations, hands-on experience, and small-group work.

Small Groups

In addition to spiritual growth opportunities and educational seminars, churches may sponsor small groups for senior adults. Groups can offer inspiration and information as well as social interaction for older people. Sunday school and discipleship programs should always structure classes for seniors. Other senior adult groups may also be organized by churches.

Participation in small groups promotes a sense of belonging and provides opportunities for social interaction. Small group involvement becomes even more important as people age since isolation and loneliness increase. Christians also need interaction with others, especially fellow believers. Support groups and senior citizen groups are often a part of church life. Involvement in these church groups contributes to the health and vitality of aging adults.

Joan and her sister Jean expressed appreciation that their mother's church sponsors so many programs for senior adults. The ministry to shut-ins includes regular phone calls, cards, and occasional visits. At Thanksgiving and Christmas, the church often delivers baskets and flowers. Sunday services are televised, providing inspiration and a continued sense of connection for those not able to attend. Churches minister more effectively to the needs of the body of believers when they include programs for senior adults.

Since senior adults often experience the same problems, they may benefit from support groups—peer-led groups of individuals seeking help to face a similar life challenge. Christian adults typically seek comfort from the Lord and counsel from His Word when suffering. Therefore, they often prefer support from other Christians and help from a Christian perspective. A wise church will provide biblically based support groups to meet the needs of senior members. Churches may provide support groups based on the common needs among senior adults:

- retirement
- widowhood

- cancer and critical illness
- grandparenting
- death and dying

In these groups, information can be provided and encouragement offered to older adults facing these challenges. Churches may also offer support groups for caregivers. People juggling responsibilities for their own families in addition to caring for parents need support as well.

Many churches have senior adult ministries, programs for older members. They involve a variety of activities and are called by many different names. Some typical names for the senior adult church groups include:

- The B.A.L.L. Club (Be Active, Live Longer)
- Keenagers
- Senior Saints
- SAM (senior adult ministries)

One church describes its program with an acrostic of its name—SENIORS.

S   spirituality
E   enrichment
N   nutrition and fitness
I   intergenerational
O   outreach
R   recreation
S   service

Senior adult programs in the church should meet the varied needs of aging members, including spiritual, physical, social, and mental. In addition to fellowships and small groups, senior ministries may sponsor a choir, offer exercise classes, and provide service opportunities. These ministries not only support seniors, they also strengthen the church. Interaction of senior adults with members of all ages stimulates the health of a church. Churches in the future must plan and budget for senior adult programs, especially as the baby boomer generation ages.

Home Visitation

Senior adult programs in the church began with homebound ministry years ago, targeted to reach shut-ins. Volunteers in the church made visits to those members who were unable to attend church due to health problems. Visits were primarily for personal enrichment and prayer support. However, visitors often shared Sunday school books, other church materials, or sermon tapes. Practical needs were also met. Groups in the church often adopted shut-ins, making visits and taking gifts. The homebound ministry kept infirm members connected to the congregation of believers and sometimes reached the unsaved for the Lord.

Home visitation continues to be an important part of senior adult church ministries. Personal visits by the senior adult minister, other church staff, deacons, Sunday school classmates, or other church members are encouraging to those unable to get out. Visits to those in the hospital, in a nursing home, or in a residence will lift their spirits. Though time consuming, the visit is a blessing also to the visitor who spends time with an older Christian. Families in the church should consider visiting shut-ins not only during the holidays but throughout the year.

Some churches or individual members hold weekly worship services or Bible studies in nursing homes or retirement centers. If members congregate in one living facility, the church ministry could be multiplied. Christians would be promoting spiritual growth and improving quality of life for other believers. Church groups should also plan parties for, play games with, and provide programs for those unable to come to church. The blessings are experienced by all, the visitors and the visited.

My mother is on an active campaign at this time to get Wednesday morning prayer meetings started at our church. She is concerned that she and many of her friends are no longer able to attend church at night. These older church members love to pray, and they want a midweek service. Mother read about a church in Alabama having a Wednesday morning prayer meeting to gather church members who could not get out at night. Mother is convinced that many seniors in our church would attend a week service, and the needs of those with limited evening outings would be met. Churches must find ways to reach members who are totally homebound as well as those with restricted access to church.

Meaningful Ministry

As more seniors live longer and enjoy better health, they want to be more involved in meaningful activity. They are not satisfied with trips to Branson and to see the fall leaves. They want trips with a purpose. Many older Christians want to serve the Lord through ongoing ministry or periodic mission projects. While senior adults can participate in any program of the church, it is even more appealing to offer programs just for them. Opportunities to serve within the church and outside in the community should be offered. Seniors can make a difference in the church and in the world as they serve others.

The church can provide programs for senior adults to participate in mentoring, ministry, and missions. It is impossible to overemphasize the importance of mentoring, the profound impact an older Christian can have on a younger one. Senior adults can mentor younger adults, teenagers, or children. Mentoring programs may pair an older woman and a younger woman in the church for the purpose of encouragement and friendship. Foster grandparent or adoption programs can provide young people with godly role models. Older adults may also be teachers in after-school tutoring or English as a second Language programs. Through relationships with younger people, senior adults can provide meaningful mentoring.

Ministry by senior adults comes in many different forms. Gifts and abilities can be used to meet the needs of others. Educational background or professional experience can be utilized in later years for ministry. Senior adults can be a part of many ministries of the local church, such as food pantry, clothing closet, tape ministry, and greeters. In addition, seniors can perform significant ministry beyond the church through disaster relief and community services.

Chuck and I recently visited a dynamic church in Naples, Florida. It was exciting to see the ministry of the gray-haired members. Though many of them had retired from their jobs and moved to Florida, those seniors had not retired from ministry. They were actively involved in the work of the church. Senior adults served as parking attendants, greeters, ushers, and counselors. A disaster relief team had just returned from work in a hurricane-ravaged area. How stimulating it is for Christians in their later years to be involved in meaningful ministry!

Senior adults can also participate in mission endeavors. They can support missions with their prayers and offerings, but seniors can also be a part of the mission work itself. Mission trips are common now for older Christians. Both missionary agencies of the Southern Baptist Convention appoint senior adults to short-term mission assignments. Older volunteers can work alongside missionaries or relieve them for a visit home. Many seniors enjoy mission experiences on the domestic or foreign fields. Often mission projects can begin right at home.

I am praying fervently that my dad will find meaningful ministry at this stage of his life. For many years, Dad was active as an evangelist. Now, his life has slowed down and he is learning how to enjoy retirement. However, it is very important for him to continue the ministry to which God has called him. Ministry for him will be different now than it was before, but Dad can still be a part of meaningful ministry. All Christians and particularly vocational ministers need to continue serving the Lord as the years pass.

No one is ever too old to mentor, minister, or be on mission! In fact, senior adults should be the largest force of missionaries, setting an example for younger Christians and reaching the lost in Jesus's name. The wealth of experience, wisdom, and faith that often abound in older persons should not be lost or under-utilized. In addition, older adults want to contribute to future generations and to feel valued because of their contributions. Churches need to recognize the vital impact of senior adults on the church and the kingdom.

The psalmist praised the Lord for the faithfulness of the righteous in Psalm 92. Scripture affirms that the faithful will flourish and be fruitful in their old age.

> The righteous thrive like a palm tree and grow like a cedar tree in Lebanon. Planted in the house of the Lord, they thrive in the courtyards of our God. They will still bear fruit in old age, healthy and green, to declare, "The Lord is just; He is my rock, and there is no unrighteousness in Him."
> —Psalm 92:12–15

The church supports older members in their later years, and older Christians support the vital ministries of the church. God's plan includes senior saints in the spread of the gospel and the work of the kingdom. God's will is for Christians of all ages to strengthen each other and for the church to minister to senior members. In doing so, God is glorified and Christians are served. Caregivers should support the work of the church, and daughters should encourage their aging mothers to remain faithful.

Mother-Daughter Reflections

1. Do you encourage spiritual growth in your mother? In what ways?

2. What sources of information and means of education provided by the church have been helpful to your mother?

3. What support systems and senior adult groups does your church offer?

4. What guidelines has your church developed for home visitation to older people?

5. In what meaningful ministry is your mother involved? How does the ministry impact her?

Chapter Fourteen

Seeking Outside Help

Today there is no need for anyone to face the challenges of caregiving alone. Help and support are available to seniors and to caregivers. Information and education are accessible to everyone. Research and referrals can identify appropriate services in the community. It is crucial for caregivers to seek outside help for themselves and their loved ones.

Seek assistance. Some people find it very hard to admit that they need help. Independence, pride, and stubbornness often discourage the needy from reaching out. However, if a person turns to others for assistance, that does not mean they are weak or helpless. Everyone will need help from others at some time. So ask for help.

A friend was shocked recently when visiting an aunt and uncle in another state. Once active adults, her relatives were now homebound with no help or support from others. Her elderly uncle had diabetes and was no longer able to get out of bed. Her aunt tried to care for him but was unable to lift him by herself. Both were desperate emotionally. They were alone and frightened. Their home was in disarray and filled with clutter. Their business affairs were out of control, and the situation seemed hopeless. The couple didn't want to burden their family, yet they didn't know where to turn for outside help. Their niece became their concerned caregiver and found help for their personal, medical, and financial needs. This story could be repeated many times. Senior adults often are unaware of outside resources available to them.

Trust advice. When outside assistance is sought, it is important to trust the advice given. Professionals who have experience with senior adults will have valuable knowledge about services. If contact is made with a reliable, qualified person or agency, you can follow their counsel with confidence. Trust the advice of outside professional sources.

During the process of finding an appropriate living arrangement for Chuck's parents, we suggested to Mom Kelley that Papa might need more care than she did. Of course, Mom wanted to live with Papa in an assisted living setting. However, as we visited different facilities, without exception, each representative suggested that the Kelleys should consider independent living for her and skilled nursing care for him. The reason was always the same—"It is our experience that the healthy spouse lives down to the level of the unhealthy spouse." It seemed better for both of them to live in a setting appropriate for their individual needs. Mom

Kelley trusted the advice of professionals and made the best decision. Though it is hard to live separately from her husband of more than 60 years, Mom Kelley depended on the counsel of professionals to make the important decision. Three years later, it is obvious to all that the professionals were right. Mom Kelley is thriving as she lives independently and Papa is well cared for by medical staff 24 hours a day.

Take action. Many older people know what to do but are hesitant to do it. Older adults often resist making difficult decisions and seem overwhelmed by change. Caregivers often wait for their loved ones to take action. However, the time comes when a decision must be made and action must be taken. Don't let fear or inertia keep you from acting. Outsiders can help loved ones get going. Professionals can also assist in the effort and serve as accountability agents for action.

My mother talked about selling her home for years. She considered other living arrangements and talked with realtors. She felt the burden of upkeep for her home and knew she needed to move. Together Mother and I discussed the pros and cons of leaving her family home. But the decision ultimately was hers. I am grateful that she talked openly with me and sought outside advice from others. However, for a long time, Mother could not take action. One evening we talked again about her future and planned to continue our dialogue in coming days. I was stunned but thrilled the next day to learn that Mother had put her home on the market and sold her house only two hours after the sign went up. Mother took action, making the best decision for herself and sparing her children from tough times.

Outside assistance is available to seniors and their caregivers. More than ever before in history, the elderly have support services and professional assistance. Though you may be new to the challenge of eldercare, the field is vast and growing. Many resources are available now and will develop in the future. This chapter will review outside services available to support you and your loved one. Professional, spiritual, relational, and financial help is available if you desire it.

Professional Help

In recent years, the field of geriatric care has expanded to include many different professionals. Their educational training and clinical experience make these professionals very valuable resources. Geriatric professionals can provide assistance with diagnosis, treatment, and management of problems typical of aging. Professional help is available in many medical centers, educational institutions, and state agencies. Begin the pursuit of help with your loved one's primary care doctor and follow recommendations to other sources.

A recent magazine advertisement by the University of Pittsburgh explained the revolutionary changes in geriatric care while also promoting their programs:

> Geriatric care starts with medical professionals from many disciplines coming together to address health issues that plague older adults. Combine this multi-talented team with the resources of a world-renowned medical center, and treatments that can revolutionize geriatric medicine begin to emerge....The ultimate goals are to discover better treatments and, in the process, use this information to redesign the approach to geriatric care. We are bridging the gap between research and clinical practice.

What a blessing to know that medical advances in geriatrics will support adults who are living longer!

While a comprehensive list of resources (books, articles, organizations, and Internet sites) is included in the back of this book, this chapter will include a brief discussion of professional resources as well as a description of special terms. Physicians are a primary source of professional help. Your loved one may see an internist, family practitioner, or gerontologist for general health needs. Specialists such as cardiologists, rheumatologists, urologists, or psychiatrists may be recommended for particular medical conditions. Other professionals may be involved in total care: psychologists; social workers; nurses; or speech, physical, occupational, or recreational therapists.

Professional organizations and agencies also offer help for the elderly. They provide literature, classes, support groups, therapy, and respite care for senior adults and their caregivers. These organizations also provide advocacy for seniors and pay for research in areas of aging. Many states have created a 211 service like 911 or 411 to provide information and referrals that include adult day care and geriatric resources. You can receive information and help from these groups.

The following agencies may be useful outside sources to help with your aging loved one:

Organizations and Agencies to Assist the Elderly
- American Association of Retired People (AARP)— www.aarp.org, 1-888-687-2277
- Alzheimer's Association—www.alz.org, 1-800-272-3900
- Eldercare Locator—www.eldercare.gov, 1-800-677-1116
- National Center on Caregiving—www.caregiver.org, 1-800-445-8106
- National Alliance for Caregiving—www.caregiving.org

A newspaper in Florida prints a weekly column under the heading "Elder Services." Senior adults and their caregivers in the community can learn about adult day care programs, meal sites, and educational programs. What a helpful service for the elderly who cannot access the Internet and may read the newspaper before they read a book or magazine. It also demonstrates that local assistance is available.

Geriatric care managers have recently emerged to coordinate services for senior adults and communicate with concerned family members. Since many Americans take care of aging relatives from afar, these professionals can help with medical, personal, social, and financial needs. Geriatric care managers are typically licensed in a field of specialization, such as social work or nursing, and may be members of the National Association of Professional Geriatric Care Managers (NAPGCM).

What does a geriatric care manager do? Here's some information from the *AARP Bulletin Online* (Dec. 2001).

- Compiles an assessment of an older person's needs and situation
- Encourages the person to accept help and provides a "plan of care" with specific recommendations
- Finds and secures services such as legal counsel, home care, nursing care, or home maintenance
- Supports and counsels family members

Our friend Dianne Boazman is a social worker who specializes in eldercare. She offered wise counsel to our family as we made decisions for the Kelleys. She and her colleagues provide geriatric care management to many clients in the New Orleans area. Sometimes they work directly for the senior adult, assisting in legal and business matters, helping with shopping and errands, monitoring medication intake, or scheduling doctor visits. In other cases, the family hires the geriatric care managers to work on their behalf. These specialized professionals are of great value now and will become even more needed as the senior population increases.

The elderly and their caregivers may be unable to utilize the resources available because of lack of understanding of the field of geriatrics or lack of awareness of the services. Professionals make recommendations and sometimes mention terms that are unfamiliar. Caregivers must become experts in gerontology in order to care adequately for their loved ones. A description of some professional terms may be helpful at this point:

- **Adult day care**—a program of medical and social services that includes socialization, activities, and supervision, provided in an outpatient setting.
- **Case management**—client assessment, identification and coordination of community resources, and follow-up monitoring of client adjustment and service provision.
- **Chore services**—household repairs, yard work, and errands.
- **Congregate meals**—meals provided in a group setting to help with nutrition and socialization.
- **Home-delivered meals**—meals delivered to the home for individuals who are unable to shop or cook for themselves.
- **Home health aide services**—assistance with health-related tasks, such as medications, exercises, and personal care.
- **Homemaker services**—household services, such as cooking, cleaning, laundry, and shopping, and escort service to accompany patients to medical appointments and elsewhere.
- **Hospice services**—medical, nursing, and social services to provide support and alleviate suffering for dying persons and their families.
- **Legal services**—assistance with legal matters, such as advance directives, guardianship, power of attorney, and transfer of assets.
- **Mental health services**—psychosocial assessment and individual and group counseling to address psychological and emotional problems of patients and families.

- **Occupational therapy**—treatment to improve functional abilities; provided by an occupational therapist.
- **Paid companion/sitter**—an individual who comes to the home to provide supervision, personal care, and socialization during the absence of the primary caregiver.
- **Personal care**—assistance with basic self-care activities, such as bathing, dressing, getting out of bed, eating, and using the bathroom.
- **Personal emergency response systems**—telephone-based systems to alert others that an individual who is alone is experiencing an emergency and needs assistance.
- **Physical therapy**—rehabilitative treatment provided by a physical therapist.
- **Protective services**—social and law enforcement services to prevent, eliminate, or remedy the effects of physical and emotional abuse or neglect.
- **Recreational services**—physical exercise, art and music therapy, parties, celebrations, and other social and recreational activities.
- **Respite care**—short-term inpatient or outpatient services intended to provide temporary relief for the caregiver.
- **Skilled nursing**—medical care provided by a licensed nurse on an inpatient basis.
- **Speech therapy**—treatment to improve or restore speech; provided by a speech therapist.
- **Supervision**—monitoring an individual's whereabouts to ensure his or her safety.
- **Telephone reassurance**—provides regular telephone calls to individuals who are isolated and often homebound.
- **Transportation**—transporting people to medical appointments, community facilities, and elsewhere.
  (List taken from *The 36-Hour Day* by Nancy Mace and Peter Rabins, page 170.)

As you can tell from this brief discussion, professional help for your aging loved one is available if you know where to look and will accept assistance. In fact, if you begin to explore options, you will find that one resource leads to another. You can also get help from spiritual advisors, friends, relatives, and financial consultants.

Spiritual Help

Christian friends and ministers are called by God to help others. Many of them have particular concern for older adults and enjoy ministering to them. It is important for your loved one to interact with spiritual leaders, to have visits from religious representatives, and to be prayed for by interested Christians. Spiritual help is available and strengthens the soul of aging individuals.

Local church pastors and other staff members should give attention to the needs and the contributions of older members. Not only are they the financial backbone of the church, they also provide invaluable wisdom and experience. Many churches have senior adult ministers to provide programs and services for seniors.

Hospitals, hospice care groups, retirement centers, and nursing homes often have chaplains who provide compassion and spiritual care. Evangelical chaplains are committed to sharing the gospel, encouraging hearts, and ministering to individuals and families in times of need. While chaplains serve the Lord in many settings (health care, law enforcement, military, prison, marketplace, etc.), many chaplains focus on care of the elderly. Personal visits, prayer times, Bible study groups, and special services led by chaplains can minister to the spiritual needs of senior adults.

Christian friends can provide the greatest source of spiritual help. Older adults are encouraged by the prayers and concern of friends. Prayer support and personal interaction strengthens older people and their caregivers. Christians need not neglect their aging friends. Cards, calls, and contacts from others offer spiritual help. Sunday school classes and church groups often reach out to the elderly, who can become isolated and feel neglected. The body of Christ is to care for one another through the passing years.

Chuck's parents and my parents have always been deeply spiritual. Each has nurtured a personal relationship with the Lord, attended church regularly, and developed strong friendships with other Christians. As they age, our parents have received spiritual help from their pastors and other church staff, chaplains, and Christian friends. Chuck's mother and my mother love the pastor of our church. They pray for him and support his ministry. In response, the pastor nurtures them spiritually through sermons, visits, and notes. Both of our mothers have benefited from the chaplaincy ministry when hospitalized for illness or surgery. Now, our parents have regular spiritual guidance from the chaplain at their retirement center, who coordinates weekly services, visits residents, and supports family members. Truly, our parents' greatest spiritual help is from Christian friends. Their days are brightened by cards and calls from longtime Christian friends. Their weeks are sprinkled with visits and lunches with new church friends. It is a blessing to see our parents receive such strong spiritual support in their later years.

Relational Help

Outside help is also available to senior adults through interaction with others. Friends and neighbors as well as family members extend love and labor to loved ones. Aging adults enjoy friendships with peers and time with contemporaries who share interests and experiences. While parents love to be with their children and grandchildren, they also like to spend time with friends and neighbors of a similar age. In addition to companionship, friends can also assist with personal care. Even if friends don't offer help, don't hesitate to ask them. Their love for your parent will compel them to help.

Volunteer assistance from friends and neighbors is an excellent resource. Most people like to help but may not know how. When you ask a friend or neighbor to care for your loved one, be sure to carefully explain her condition. Clarify what tasks you expect the volunteer to perform. Tell them how to relate to your loved one and how to assist them. Help them feel comfortable while helping, and don't make too many demands on their time. Consider individuals who live close by and who can help with specific needs. When possible, give advance notice and anticipate potential problems. Be sure not to criticize what volunteers do, and always express appreciation for their help.

I am grateful for the support of friends and neighbors who care for Mom Kelley. Her relational needs are met by family as well as through daily social interaction with others. She loves her weekly grocery shopping excursions with neighbors and daily lunches with girlfriends. My mother is also a tremendous support to Mom Kelley. They have become dear friends and love spending time together. Since my mother still drives and gets out often, she offers to run errands for Mom Kelley. While my tendency as the primary caregiver is to feel responsible for all the support, I realize that Mother enjoys helping, and Mom Kelley needs interaction with friends of her own age. The moms enjoy time together when Mother drives them to church or takes Mom Kelley to the eye doctor. Friends and neighbors can provide valuable relational help.

Many groups train "special visitors" to relate personally to adults with similar conditions. They provide understanding and information as well as social interaction. Adult day care programs offer not only supervision and recreational activities, but also socialization among peers. You alone cannot meet all the relational needs of your loved one. They can benefit from regular interaction with other family members, friends, and neighbors. You can facilitate relational help by organizing visits and encouraging interaction. Your loved one can also receive outside financial help.

Financial Help

Management of personal finances is often overwhelming to individuals. Add to that the oversight of a loved one's financial affairs and the task seems impossible. Financial help should be secured to handle business and legal issues facing your aging loved one. Both you and yours will be more confident in consultation with financial professionals.

A financial advisor will provide assistance to help develop a budget, oversee expenses, and manage investments. Many senior adults live on a fixed income with limited assets and variable investments. Some have prepared for retirement, while others seem ill-prepared financially for the later stage of life. Since finances are such a personal matter, caregivers benefit from the expertise of an objective professional. If your loved one doesn't already have a financial advisor, you would be wise to secure one.

Many Christians seek biblically based counseling about financial affairs. Christian financial services are available and can help older adults manage their money. Ronald Blue & Co. provides biblically based financial services online and from their regional offices around the country. Their financial services for individuals or organizations include the following:
- financial and estate planning
- investment analysis and management
- complete tax preparation

- business services
- retirement planning
- charitable giving strategic development

For more information, see their Web site (www.ronblue.com) or call 1-800-841-0362.

Larry Burkett taught biblically based financial principles in his books and through his ministry for many years. Since his death in 2003, his services continue through the ministry he founded, Crown Financial Ministries (www.crown.org).

Christians can be assured of godly money management through biblically based financial counseling. It is important to develop trust and confidence in your financial advisor.

Accountants can assist the elderly in securing eligible tax breaks. General information is provided by the Internal Revenue Service in a publication entitled "Tax Benefits for Older Americans." In addition, insurance agents can clarify coverage of policies. Health and long-term care insurance may pay for some medically related services. Disability or life insurance may also be a resource. Some policies waive premiums for disabled clients. Monetary savings and financial income may be available from insurance as well.

Medicare provides the greatest financial assistance to senior adults at the present time. Medicare income is received by individuals and spouses over the age of 65 who have contributed to the fund. Information is available online (www.medicare.gov) or by phone (1-800-MEDICARE). Medicaid services are also available to the disabled. While federal and state laws shape Medicaid, some states offer payment for nursing home care. For information about Medicaid, see the Centers for Medicare and Medicaid Services Web site (www.cms.hhs.gov) or call 1-877-267-2323. As years pass and expenses increase, financial assistance from all means is helpful to senior adults. Other forms of state, federal, and private resources may be secured for your loved one if you pursue financial help.

Legal professionals can also offer financial help for you and your loved one. Wills, power of attorney, and living wills must be executed by attorneys. In addition, they can advise you and your loved ones concerning legal rights and represent you if rights are violated. Some attorneys specialize in law relating to aging and caregiving. A list of credentialed lawyers is available from the National Academy of Elder Law Attorneys (www.naela.org, [520] 881-4005). This information also may be helpful to you.

For More Information
- National Association of Professional Geriatric Care Managers—www.caremanager.org, (520) 881-8008
- Medicare—www.medicare.gov, 1-800-MEDICARE
- Medicaid—www.cms.hhs.gov, 1-877-267-2323
- National Academy of Elder Law Attorneys—www.naela.org, (520) 881-4005

Many other outside resources are available to help your loved one and to support you. This chapter presents a limited number of resources that provide professional, spiritual, relational, and financial help. As you continue this journey of caregiving, you will learn more about the needs of your loved one and the assistance available to you. Don't feel alone. Help is on the way!

Mother-Daughter Reflections

1. What outside help have you secured for your loved one?

2. What professional services are available to you and your loved one?

3. What spiritual encouragement does your loved one receive on a regular basis?

4. What social interaction does your loved one have on a daily, weekly, or monthly basis?

5. What financial assistance have you sought to help manage your loved one's business affairs?

Chapter Fifteen

Discussing the Future

There are several topics considered by most people to be taboo in polite conversation. Society avoids talking about religion and politics since people have such strong, often opposing, viewpoints. For families, there are several other subjects to be overlooked in table talk—dependence, disability, and death. It is hard for loved ones to discuss topics so dismal and dreaded. However, open discussion and honest input are essential for healthy family functioning. The Bible also shows the need for Christians to talk about the important matters of life and death.

Christians are to talk about their faith in God, sharing the gospel with unbelievers to draw them to salvation. While confrontation and coercion are not appropriate, Christians should confidently testify of God's work in their lives. Talk about religion should flow spontaneously from the lips of people walking closely with the Lord. In fact, Christians can comfortably talk about the future without fear of the unknown. The promise of His presence during life and heaven after death give Christians hope and comfort. Truly, Christians know who holds the future—God. And they know He strengthens and sustains them when they are facing times of dependence, disability, or even death.

Families need to discuss the future as soon as possible. It is never too early to talk about personal convictions and desires concerning life and death. For many, it is too late when illness strikes or death comes suddenly. In the midst of the crisis is no time to make important decisions. Undue pressure is put on family members to make decisions for a loved one. Unnecessary hardship faces family members who disagree about difficult decisions. Innocent loved ones may even be taken advantage of by selfish family members with personal agendas. Everyone is helped when these tough topics are addressed before a time of need.

While it is never too early to discuss dependence, disability, and death, it can be too late. The risks become greater as time passes and loved ones age. Unfortunately, even young people should consider the future since life is uncertain. Just last week, a precious 31-year-old friend was tragically killed in a car accident. Death and funeral plans had never been discussed by this young woman and her family, so they were faced with many decisions while dealing with their own personal grief. Some comfort was experienced by the knowledge that Stephanie was in heaven. During the funeral, family and friends recalled her personal signature on correspondence—"In His hands." She had always been in God's hands, but after her sudden death,

Stephanie was truly in His hands. Her death came without time for preparation and planning, but Stephanie was prepared to die because of her personal relationship with Jesus Christ.

In this chapter, long-range possibilities for the future will be discussed. While every person's life and death is different, several scenarios may occur. Many people become dependent or disabled, and death is inevitable for all. It is helpful for families to express personal perspectives concerning dependence, disability, and death.

Dependence

One of the most important life skills that parents teach their children is independence. From birth, infants and then children rely solely on others to provide for their needs. As they grow, children learn from their parents and other concerned adults how to make decisions and become self-reliant. For most of life people live independently, caring for themselves and those dependent on them. Some people are never able to function independently. In other cases, independence is cut short by illness or injury. But most adults live independently. Therefore, it is difficult for self-reliant people to become dependent on others.

Families need to talk about the ways they relate to each other. Individual personalities as well as life circumstances often determine how independently family members can live. Consideration should be given to how each person would respond if forced to depend on others for daily living. The time will come when someone in the family will become totally dependent on another. Previous conversations can assist when future needs arise.

The shift from independence to dependence usually occurs when the loved one is physically or mentally unable to take care of personal needs. When one cannot care for herself, outside help is needed and dependent living begins. As long as one can manage dressing, feeding, taking medications, and other daily living skills, she can remain independent. Basic life skills are necessary for independent living.

When an individual becomes dependent, attitudes as well as actions are impacted. Activities can be assumed by another person, but the dependent individual may find it difficult to manage her own attitude. Discussing the dependent lifestyle in advance may improve attitudes. The care receiver should feel gratitude and respond cooperatively. The caregiver should feel blessed and act reliably. Negative attitudes will further burden both of them. Talk openly with your loved ones about their wishes for personal help in the future.

Many people feel that they are forced to be dependent. They may resent their helpless state and may resist assistance. Cooperation is needed. In reality, the caregiver is dependent on their loved one to receive care. If older people refuse the support that is offered, they restrict the caregiver and deny the blessings of giving. An aging parent's greatest gift to a child is to accept dependence and receive care graciously.

Older people who are dependent are not powerless. In fact, they can remain powerful in many areas of life. Christopher de Vinck discussed this paradox in his book, *The Power of the Powerless*. Part of the job of aging well is to recognize the difference between what can be done and what care is needed. Senior adults should continue doing what they can do as long as possible, then they must accept care when they can no longer perform a task. Families benefit from talking about the progression from independence to dependence. The balance between independence and dependence is both dynamic and delicate, always changing and needing constant adjustment. In aging, the powerless can remain powerful when they balance this tension successfully.

My mother is still a very active, independent 79-year-old woman. Often when we are together, I offer to perform a task for her. She defensively responds, "I can do it." Mother sees many of her friends becoming dependent and wants to remain independent herself. While I appreciate her determination, I would also love to do things for her. Sometimes I respond, "I know you *can* do it, but will you please *let* me do it for you?" Mother and I are beginning to discuss the future as we navigate these encounters. I pray that we will be better prepared when she becomes dependent.

Disability

The 2004 US census identified 54 million disabled men, women, and children. While many disabled individuals are young, most are 65 years of age or older. The likelihood of physical or mental disability increases with age. Abilities decrease due to illness or aging. Therefore, disability must be considered a future possibility for many older people. Families should discuss options for care if disability occurs.

Disabled people today have many legal rights and many financial resources. Awareness has improved and protections have emerged for the disabled population. Respect and recognition are given to those who were previously rejected or ignored by society. If your loved one becomes physically or mentally disabled, your responsibility is to insure her best interests. Get help for your disabled family member or friend.

In her book *The Hard Questions for Adult Children and Their Aging Parents*, Susan Piver asks several important questions to help families consider these matters before facing them:

1. Whom would you like to make health care decisions for you if you are not capable of making them yourself?
2. Are there any everyday tasks you would like for us to look after should you become too infirm to do so on your own?

3. If you can't take care of yourself physically, where would you prefer to live?

4. If you become ill or depressed, are there others—family, friends, clergy—whom you would like for me to ask to visit you?

5. What would you expect to happen to your quality of life if you became disabled?

Families would also benefit from answering the other questions compiled by Susan Piver in her book.

Long-term disability and decline give family members the opportunity to unite around decisions for the loved one: sudden death denies such opportunity. Though difficult to discuss, families should consider a person's preferences if the future holds dependence or disability. Assisting a living relative is as necessary as grieving a dying relative.

As you and your family discuss the future and deal with disability, keep these suggestions in mind:

- **Think ahead.** Try to anticipate future challenges that may arise and develop options in advance.

- **Be prepared for the unexpected.** Surprises happen not only in events, but with people. Don't let the unexpected happenings upset you.

- **Accept that there is no one answer.** There may be several options or multiple answers. Don't unrealistically expect to always know the correct answer.

- **Respect opinions of others.** Everyone deserves respect. Even if your opinions differ, you should respect the person.

- **Focus on the patient.** Keep in mind your loved one's needs and values. Don't impose your own ideas and don't encourage others to pursue their paths without regard for the loved one's wishes and needs. The patient matters most.

"It's not about me" has become a familiar saying among Christians. How true! It is always about God—His will and plan for our lives. It is about others—their needs and desires. It is not about me and my wishes. Family members must avoid selfishness when caring for loved ones. It is all about the patient—your parent, your loved one, your friend.

Unfortunately, the elderly and disabled are often taken advantage of by selfish relatives or commercial scams. Your loved ones must be protected from exploitation. Those who would pursue their own personal interests should be denied contact with the disabled and even prosecuted for their crime. There is a vulnerability within older adults to believe that everyone cares for them sincerely.

Mom Kelley can be gullible and often believes that the solicitations of others are sincere. She naively thinks that a letter written to her by a telemarketer is a personal invitation written individually to her. She often feels that she must give to every telephone solicitor. We are grateful that she talks with us first, and we can try to clarify the matter. However, many elderly and disabled are unfortunately the target of people selfishly interested in only themselves. Talk clearly with your loved one about the challenges of the disabled.

Death

Death is not typically a pleasant or comfortable topic. Many people dislike discussions about death and even ignore or deny the possibility of dying. However, the saying is true: "two things are certain in life—death and taxes." Since death is inevitable, we might as well talk about it.

As medical advances have been made, the topic of death has disappeared from conversations. In earlier history, death was rampant due to disease and injury. Thus, it was a common topic of discussion. However, the dramatic improvement of medical care today prevents many early deaths. Diseases are diagnosed earlier, resulting in better outcomes. People with serious conditions often survive because of expert medical treatment. It is easy to think that doctors can cure any affliction. Death does not seem imminent, and thus it need not be discussed.

Though death may not be a conscious part of daily life, the reality that life will end must be considered. Caregivers will benefit from honest discussions about death with their loved ones, and the elderly are better prepared to face the future if they talk openly about it. While there is no need to become morbid in thinking about death, it is best not to avoid the subject. Matters concerning death should be discussed openly.

Since my husband's father owned a funeral home for 42 years, Chuck's family talks naturally about death. Papa Kelley remembers people for whom he conducted funerals. Mom Kelly reads the obituaries in the daily paper, and the Kelley kids talk to each other about funeral plans. I am grateful for their healthy attitudes about death. The Kelleys have helped me better understand death and relax when discussing the subject with my loved ones.

Concerning death, adult children should talk with their parents about dying wishes, dying victory, and dying dignity. It is important to discuss last wishes with your parents and to complete appropriate legal documents. Living wills state how a person wants to be treated in the event of terminal illness and impending death. Specific requests can be made to "not resuscitate," or withhold heroic measures. Loved ones can clearly specify whether they wish a feeding tube to be used to sustain life. Permission to donate organs can be granted. Preferences should be discussed with family members and physicians, and formal papers should be filed with a lawyer and a hospital.

The Terri Schiavo case in 2005 tragically focused the public's attention on the right to die. Her parents and her husband disagreed about life support. Each family member purported to represent her wishes, though she left no legal documentation. The courts decided her fate after years of debate. The Schiavo case should convince all adults to make their wishes known clearly and completely. Christians need to state their dying wishes and rejoice in their dying victory.

The promise of heaven gives another reason to celebrate death. The Bible paints a beautiful picture of heaven. It is the dwelling place of God and the eternal home of all His children. Heaven is a place...

- prepared for believers (John 14:1–4)
- without sorrow or sin (Revelation 21:1–7)
- where loved ones recognize each other (1 John 3:2)
- of beauty and glory (Revelation 21:22–26)
- where bodies are perfected (1 Corinthians 15:51–57)

Christians can rejoice in death, the beginning of eternal life in the presence of God. There is great comfort in celebrating the life of a loved one and believing in the place where eternal life continues.

Christians can also die with dignity. When possible and for as long as possible, your loved one needs to be treated with honor and respect in every way. She should be made comfortable and be cared for in the best possible ways. You should work with doctors and other health care professionals to try to manage her pain. If possible, determine where she wants to die. Some people prefer spending their final days in a home or hospice rather than a hospital. In many ways, the hospice movement has given dignity to death. Hospice provides a safe, loving, supportive environment for individuals who are dying and their families.

It is also helpful to talk with your loved one about the plans surrounding death. You could simply ask, "When it comes time for you to die, what do you want to happen at the end?" Most people want to be with the ones they love when they die. While it is hard to witness death, it is a privilege to be present when someone dies. Children are truly blessed to be with their parents as they pass from this earth and enter the presence of God. Often, a person waits to see a loved one or seeks their permission to die. Many Christians relate precious experiences as they said farewell to their loved ones. Some have read Scripture aloud or sang favorite hymns as their parent slipped away. Others held hands and recalled sweet memories. All were comforted by the presence of loved ones. Daughters should make every effort to be with their mothers at the time of death. It will be meaningful for both dying mother and caring daughter.

A high school friend recently shared with me the details of her mother's death. Debbie had tenderly cared for her aging mother and knew when her time came to die. She described that tender moment:

> When it was time for Mom to pass on, I knew her so well that I predicted the moment she would go and made certain that my brother and sister came in town to be there. I knew her so well that it was clear to me when she would go on. When my brother got in town and stood by her bed, she told him, "I've been waiting for you to get here." She died hours later with all her children by her side.

Debbie was blessed to be present as her beloved mother died with dignity, surrounded by those she loved.

Another topic for discussion with aging parents is their funeral plans. Be sure to ask about formal arrangements.

Some people purchase funeral services and buy cemetery plots before the time of death. In addition, loved ones may have thoughts about the memorial service. Consideration should be given to Scripture and songs. Participants in the funeral and details for the program should be identified. Mom Kelley actually has a "funeral file" with personal notes and sample programs to help plan both her and Papa Kelley's own services. Discussion of funeral arrangements can guarantee the loved one's wishes are granted and comfort family members at their time of loss.

Jacob's last days are recorded in Genesis 47–50. Knowing his own death was imminent, Jacob called for his sons, grandsons, and their families. He made requests about his burial to Joseph and conferred a blessing on his family. Jacob passed along his legacy of faith as he prepared to die. Christians also often desire to pass along their legacy of faith at the time of death.

While the topics of dependence, disability, and death may always be difficult to discuss with our loved ones, open communication expresses the older person's wishes and lessens the caregiver's responsibilities. Christians can be confident that God is in control even when life is fading. We know that dependence, disability, and death are overcome by the sovereign power of God. Try to talk honestly and openly with your mother about the future before you face a crisis.

Raising Moms

Adult daughters caring for their aging mothers often have the privilege of providing their primary care. You will be helped if you understand the senior generation and appreciate the mother-daughter relationship. You will meet her needs if you learn to deal with decline and make hard decisions. You will grow stronger if you build a new relationship with your mother and maintain open communication. Your family will be nurtured if you facilitate family dynamics and encourage reconciliation. Your mother will be content as you foster independence and encourage new friendships. You should follow biblical teachings, heed practical advice, involve church support, and seek outside help as you care for your mother. You should discuss the future honestly, talking openly with your mother about dependence, disability, and death.

It is my prayer that you will enjoy the blessing of "raising moms." Though the challenges may be great, you have the blessing of past childhood memories, the present power of the Holy Spirit, and the future promise of God's "Well done, My good and faithful servant!" So be faithful, dear friend, as you care for your mother in her later years. Don't grow weary in doing good, but trust Him daily for wisdom and strength.

My life has been doubly blessed as I have the privilege of caring for two moms—my mother and my mother-in-law. Their lives of faith are powerful testimonies to me. Their positive attitudes and sweet spirits glorify God daily. Their unconditional love and sincere gratitude motivate me to keep on serving. Their daughter truly rises up and calls each of them *blessed* (Proverbs 31:28). I pray that my life will be the same witness of God's grace that is demonstrated by my moms, whom I love and honor in my service to them. As they have raised me in the Lord, I now care for them and teach others to serve unselfishly. God bless you in your journey of caregiving!

Mother-Daughter Reflections

1. What topics about the future have you discussed openly with your mother?

2. How would your mother want to be treated if she became dependent upon you or others?

3. What are your mother's desires for herself if she becomes physically or mentally disabled?

4. What plans has your mother made for her death and her funeral service?

5. How does your faith affect your views about the future and the impending challenges?

Epilogue

Hurricane Katrina hit the city of New Orleans and the Gulf Coast on Monday, August 29, 2005. It was a fierce storm of catastrophic proportions. Coastal areas were washed away by the storm surge. Roofs were blown away and windows were blown out by category 5 winds. About 85% of my hometown of New Orleans was flooded when the levees broke.

The storm changed the lives of millions of people. Hundreds of people lost their lives and thousands lost their homes. The United States experienced the greatest displacement of people since the Civil War. Communities in New Orleans were left like ghost towns, and the beautiful campus of the New Orleans Baptist Theological Seminary was significantly damaged.

Chuck and I had the responsibility of protecting ourselves and the seminary, as well as securing the safety of our parents. My mother evacuated from New Orleans before the storm hit. Chuck and I were asked to evacuate by the seminary administration the day before landfall. But the Kelleys stayed at Lambeth House in New Orleans through the storm, accompanied by our family friend Vanee Daure. They fared well during the winds, but when the levees broke, they also had to evacuate the city. God got them out safely.

For four months, Chuck and I lived temporarily in Atlanta to continue the work of the seminary from our extension center there. My mother stayed with my sister in Alabama, while the Kelleys stayed with their eldest daughter and her husband in Fort Worth, Texas. Once residents of the same town, we were displaced to three different states, separated by many miles. We missed our lives and our closeness to each other. Many residents of New Orleans and the affected areas were also displaced and separated from family.

Many senior adults who had never left New Orleans were forced from their homes by floodwaters. Suddenly homeless, they sought immediate relief in shelters and longer-term housing with relatives. Thousands of families accepted the challenge and instantly became caregivers for their aging loved ones. A new phenomenon in elder care emerged. In the aftermath of Hurricane Katrina, families wrote a new book on caregiving in times of natural disaster.

A feature article in *USA Today* entitled "Thrust Into the Caregiver Role" (September 22, 2005) addressed the unique challenges of these persons who were instantly turned into caregivers. Hurricane evacuations forced families to find help, and quickly. The elderly who were often cared for in specialized facilities found themselves in crowded homes with family members. Concerned relatives who may have had little regular contact with their loved ones found themselves responsible and unprepared to care for their ill or frail elders. Suddenly, the needs of the elderly and their new caregivers have emerged and influenced the field of elder care.

Morie Pierce, a single mom in Golden, Colorado, learned about caregiving due to disaster when her 88-year-old grandmother, forced from her home in Slidell, Louisiana, moved in with Morie and her three children, as well as a dog, a cat, a lizard, hermit crabs, frogs, and fish. Though she works daily as communications director for Colorado's AARP, Morie was not prepared for the challenges of caregiving. She said, "It's very different to go from a situation of being in an elderly person's home where they have everything they need…to having that person in your home with a myriad of health needs and all of a sudden you're the novice caregiver." She received on-the-job training in senior adult caregiving while also caring for the needs of her own family.

In the midst of the tragedy caused by Hurricane Katrina, there were blessings. For some, displacement created opportunities for family togetherness. Many people spent time with family members they are rarely able to visit. Our family was blessed by our displacement even though we New Orleanians missed each other. My mother spent extended time with my sister and her four boys. They shared time together, and Mother helped with chores around the house. Since my mother returned to her own home, my sister misses her helper and my nephews miss their Mimi. Dad and Mom Kelley have spent time with two daughters and their families while in Fort Worth. Chuck and I enjoyed the retirement center in Atlanta where we have lived, surrounded by other gray-haired moms!

The greatest blessing of all is that we are safe and, after four months, we have been reunited in our homes and together in our beloved city of New Orleans! We have been strengthened by the love and prayers of family and friends. We await the work of the Lord in the city "that care forgot!"

Additional Resources

Books

Anderson-Ellis, Eugenia, and Marsha Dryan. *Aging Parents and You*. New York: Master Media, 1988.

Armstrong, Mary Vaughn. *Caregiving for Your Loved Ones*. Elgin, IL: David C. Cook, 1990.

Arn, Win, and Charles Arn. *Live Long and Love It!* Wheaton, IL: Tyndale House, 1991.

Barg, Gary. *The Fearless Caregiver: How to Get the Best Care for Your Loved One and Still Have a Life of Your Own*. Sterling, VA: Capital, 2003.

Barna, George. *The Future of the American Family*. Chicago: Moody Press, 1993.

Bathauer, Ruth M. *Parent Care: A Guide to Help Adult Children Provide Care and Support for Their Aging Parents*. Ventura, CA: Regal Books, 1990.

Beard, Patricia. *Good Daughters: Loving Our Mothers as They Age*. Lebanon, IN: Warner Books, 1999.

Cadmus, Robert R. *Caring for Your Aging Parents: A Concerned, Complete Guide for Children of the Elderly*. Old Tappan, NJ: Prentice-Hall, 1984.

Carroll, Jackson W., and Wade Clark Roof. *Bridging Divided Worlds: Generational Cultures in Congregations*. San Francisco: Jossey-Bass, 2002.

Cooper, Joan Hunter, ed. *The Fourteen Friends Guide to Eldercaring*. Sterling, VA: Capital, 1999.

Crichton, Jean. *The Age Care Sourcebook: A Resource Guide for the Aging and Their Families*. New York: Simon and Schuster, 1987.

Deane, Barbara. *Caring for Your Aging Parents: When Love Is Not Enough*. Colorado Springs: Nav Press, 1989.

Delehanty, Hugh, and Elinor Ginzler. *Caring for Your Parents: The Complete AARP Guide*. New York: Bantam Books, 2005.

Dychtwald, Ken, and Joe Flower. *Age Wave: The Challenges and Opportunities of an Aging America*. Los Angeles, CA: Jeremy P. Tarcher, Inc., 1989.

Ellison, Edna, and Tricia Scribner. *Woman to Woman: Preparing Yourself to Mentor*. Birmingham, AL: New Hope, 2005.

Fingerman, Karen. *Aging Mothers and Their Adult Daughters: A Study in Mixed Emotions*. New York: Springer Publishing Company, 2001.

Gangel, Kenneth O., and James C. Wilhoit, eds. *The Christian Educator's Handbook on Adult Education*. Grand Rapids, MI: Baker Books, 1998.

Gibson, Dennis, and Ruth Gibson. *The Sandwich Years: When Your Kids Need Friends and Your Parents Need Parenting*. Grand Rapids, MI: Baker Book House, 1991.

Gilliam, Vicki L. *Forty Days of Care for the Caregiver*. Enumclaw, WA: Wine Press Publishing, 2004.

Gillies, John. *A Guide to Caring for and Coping with Aging Parents*. Nashville: Thomas Nelson Publishers, 1981.

Goldman, Connie. *The Gifts of Caregiving*. Minneapolis, MN: Fairview Press, 2002.

Green, Tracy, and Todd Temple. *52 Ways to Show Aging Parents You Care*. Nashville: Thomas Nelson Publishers, 1992.

Guthrie, Donna. *Grandpa Doesn't Know It's Me: A Family Adjusts to Alzheimer's Disease*. New York: Human Sciences Press, 1986.

Hargrave, Terry D. *Loving Your Parents When They Can No Longer Love You*. Grand Rapids, MI: Zondervan, 2005.

Ilardo, Joseph A., and Carole R. Rothman. *I'll Take Care of You: A Practical Guide for Family Caregivers*. Oakland, CA: New Harbinger, 1999.

Jones-Lee, Anita. *The Complete Guide to Elder Care*. Hauppauge, NY: Barron's Educational Series, 1998.

Lancaster, Lynne C., and David Stillman. *When Generations Collide: Who They Are. Why They Clash. How to Solve the Generational Puzzle at Work.* New York: Harper Business, 2002.

Levy, Michael T. *Parenting Mom and Dad: A Caring Guide for the Grown-Up Children of Aging Parents.* New York: Prentice Hall Press, 1991.

Lewis, Carole, and Cara Symank. *The Mother-Daughter Legacy: How a Mother's Love Shapes a Daughter's Life.* Ventura, CA: Regal Books, 2004.

Mace, Nancy L., and Peter V. Rabins. *The 36-Hour Day: A Family Guide to Caring for Persons with Alzheimer Disease, Related Dementing Illnesses, and Memory Loss in Later Life.* Baltimore: The John Hopkins University Press, 1999.

Mall, E. Jane. *Caregiving: How to Care for Your Elderly Mother and Stay Sane.* New York: Ballantine Books, 1990.

MacLean, Helene. *Caring for Your Parents: A Sourcebook of Options and Solutions for Both Generations.* Garden City, NY: Doubleday, 1987.

McIntosh, Gary L. *One Church, Four Generations: Understanding and Reaching All Ages in Your Church.* Grand Rapids, MI: Baker Books, 2002.

McIntosh, Gary L. *Three Generations: Riding the Waves of Change in Your Church.* Grand Rapids, MI: Fleming H. Revell, 1995.

McLeod, Beth W., ed. *And Thou Shalt Honor: The Caregiver's Companion.* Emmaus, PA: Rodale, 2002.

Morris, Virginia. *How to Care for Aging Parents.* New York: Workman Publishing Company, 2004.

Northrup, Christiane. *Mother-Daughter Wisdom: Creating a Legacy of Physical and Emotional Health.* New York: Bantam Books, 2005.

Patterson, Dorothy Kelley. *The Family: Unchanging Principles for Changing Times.* Nashville: Broadman and Holman, 2002.

Patterson, Dorothy Kelley, and Rhonda Harrington Kelley, eds. *The New King James Woman's Study Bible.* Nashville: Thomas Nelson, 1995.

Piver, Susan. *The Hard Questions for Adult Children and Their Aging Parents: 100 Essential Questions for Facing the Future Together, with Courage and Compassion.* New York: Gotham Books, 2004.

Rhodes, Linda Colvin. *The Complete Idiot's Guide to Caring for Aging Parents.* Royersford, PA: Alpha Publishing, 2000.

Riekse, Robert J., and Henry Holstege. *The Christian Guide to Parent Care.* Wheaton, IL: Tyndale House Publishers, 1992.

Robertson, Betty Benson. *TLC for Aging Parents: A Practical Guide.* Kansas City, MO: Beacon Hill Press, 1992.

Rushford, Patricia H. *The Help, Hope, and Cope Book for People with Aging Parents.* Old Tappan, NJ: Fleming H. Revel, 1985.

Satow, Roberta. *Doing the Right Thing: Taking Care of Your Elderly Parents Even If They Didn't Take Care of You.* New York: Penguin Group, 2005.

Sell, Charles M. *Transitions Through Adult Life.* Grand Rapids, MI: Zondervan Publishing House, 1985.

Shelley, Florence D., and Jane Otten. *When Your Parents Grow Old.* New York: Harper and Row, 1988.

Shriver, Maria. *What's Happening to Grandpa?* New York: Little, Brown and Company, 2004.

Silverstone, Barbara, and Helen Hyman. *You and Your Aging Parent.* New York: Harper and Row, 1988.

Sowers, Laura. *Twice Blessed: Encouragement for the Caregiver and the Carereceiver.* Nashville: Broadman-Holman Publishers, 2005.

Stafford, Tim. *As Our Years Increase: Loving, Caring, Preparing: A Guide.* Grand Rapids, MI: Zondervan Publishing House, 1989.

Stagg, Frank. *The Bible Speaks on Aging.* Nashville: Broadman Press, 1981.

Strauss, William, and Neil Howe. *Generations: The History of America's Future, 1584 to 2069.* New York: William Morrow, 1991.

Stubblefield, Jerry M. *A Church Ministering to Adults.* Nashville, TN: Broadman Press, 1986.

Tannen, Deborah. *You're Wearing That? Understanding Mothers and Daughters in Conversation.* New York: Random, 2006.

Vogel, Linda Jane. *The Religious Education of Older Adults.* Birmingham, AL: Religious Education Press, 1984.

Zabbia, Kim Howes. *Painted Diaries: A Mother and Daughter's Experience Through Alzheimer's.* Minneapolis: Fairview Press, 1996.

Zukerman, Rachelle. *Eldercare for Dummies.* Hoboken, NJ: Wiley, 2003.

Articles

Atkins, Dale. "Setting Limits: Just How Much Should We Do for Our Parents?" *AARP Magazine* (May–June 2005).

Colon, Suzan. "Care for the Caregiver." *Cooking Light* (September 2005).

Delehanty, Hugh. "The Care Dividend." *AARP Magazine* (May–June 2005).

Grossman, Cathy Lynn. "Time for Loved Ones to Talk." *USA Today,* March 24, 2005, 6D.

Jayson, Sharon. "Caregiving Will Put Boomer Marriages to Test." *USA Today,* June 23, 2005, 10D.

Klass, Perri. "Why Mothers Are a Girl's Best Friend." *Ladies Home Journal* (May 2004).

Kornblum, Janet. "Caregiving Magazines Are Filling a Need." *USA Today*, June 13, 2005, 7D.

Kornblum, Janet. "Grief Knows No Bounds Over Alzheimer's Course." *USA Today*, June 23, 2004, 11D.

Kornblum, Janet. "A Nation of Caregivers." *USA Today*, April 6, 2004, 6D.

Kornblum, Janet. "Sons, Daughters and Caregivers." *USA Today*, February 17, 2004, 1D.

Levine, Irene, and Betsy Rubiner. "Caring Across the Miles." *Better Homes and Gardens* (April 2005).

Milk, Leslie. "Bringing Mom Home." *Washingtonian* 35 (October 1999).

Miller, Sue. "Watching Dad Disappear." *People* (April 14, 2003).

O'Brien, Kathleen. "More Workers Use Family Leave to Care for Parents." *The Times Picayune*, April 25, 2004, E–8.

Owens, Virginia. "What Shall We Do with Mother?" *Books & Culture: A Christian Review* 5 (July–August 1999).

Plutowski, Shelley. "Understanding Mother-Daughter Relationships." *Mayo Clinic Health Information* (October 25, 2000).

Rosenfeld, Isadore. "When It's a Matter of Life or Death." *Parade* (May 22, 2005).

Scelfo, Julie. "The Keys to Caregiving." *Newsweek* (June 21, 2004).

Shaw, Gina. "Our Mothers, Ourselves: Mother-Daughter Relationships." *Discovery Health* http://health.discovery.com/centers/womens/daughter.html.

Sheehan, Nancy W., and Laura M. Donorfio. "Efforts to Create Meaning in the Relationship Between Aging Mothers and Their Caregiving Daughters." *Journal of Aging Studies* 13 (Summer 1999).

Skelton, Vonda Skinner. "Can We Talk? Tough Questions to Ask Your Parents." *Christian Single* (May 2005).

Organizations

Administration on Aging—comprehensive overview of a wide variety of topics, programs, and services related to aging for older individuals, caregivers, or community service providers.
> Web site—www.aoa.gov
> Phone—(202) 619-0724

AgeNet—solutions for better aging with information on health, drugs, legal assistance, insurance, financial aid, and products.
> Web site—www.agenet.com
> Phone—1-888-405-4242

Aging Network Services—provides direction and hope for aging adults, even in the most difficult of circumstances.
> Web site—www.agingnets.com
> Phone—(301) 657-4329

Alzheimer's Association—support services, educational materials, and a 24-hour hotline for families of individuals with Alzheimer's disease.
>Web site—www.alz.org
>Phone—1-800-272-3900

American Academy of Hospice and Palliative Medicine—advocacy group with services and information links.
>Web site—www.aahpm.org

American Association of Retired People (AARP)—resource for senior adults; provides information on topics such as end-of-life issues, grief and loss, and legal issues.
>Web site—www.aarp.org
>Phone—1-888-OUR-AARP (1-888-687-2277)

Caregiving.com—provides information on managing the stress, making the decisions, and discovering the meaning of caring for your aging loved one; offers support groups, coaches, newsletters, book club, and weekly encouragement.
>Web site—www.caregiving.com

Eldercare Locator—public service of the US Administration on Aging, which connects older Americans and their caregivers with sources of information on senior services; links those who need assistance with state and local area agencies on aging and community-based organizations.
>Web site—www.eldercare.gov
>Phone—1-800-677-1116

ElderWeb—finds in-home care for your loved one with various needs.
>Web site—www.elderweb.com

Family Caregiver Alliance—provides information, education, services, research, and advocacy, as well as supports and sustains important work with families nationwide caring for loved ones with chronic, disabling health conditions.

    Web site—www.caregiver.org

    Phone—(415) 434-3388 or 1-800-445-8106

Medicare—provides information on Medicare coverage, long-term care resources, nursing home comparisons, and a physician directory.

    Web site—www.medicare.gov

    Phone—1-800-MEDICARE (1-800-633-4227)

National Alliance for Caregiving—provides support to families, caregivers, and professionals who help them and increases public awareness of issues facing family caregivers.

    Web site—www.caregiving.org

National Association of Professional Geriatric Care Managers—works privately with older adults and their families to create a plan of care that meets the needs of the older adult; identifies resources and options available to meet those needs.

    Web site—www.caremanager.org

    Phone—(520) 881-8008

National Council on the Aging—national network of organizations and individuals dedicated to improving the health and independence of older persons and increasing their continuing contributions to communities, society, and future generations.

    Web site—www.ncoa.org

    Phone—(202) 479-1200 or 1-800-424-9046

National Family Caregiver Support Program—educates caregivers who care for aged loved ones, improving the quality of life of caregiving families.

    Web site—http://www.aoa.gov/prof/aoaprog/caregiver/carefam/carefam.asp

    Phone—(202) 619-0724

National Family Caregivers Association—supports, educates, and represents those caring for chronically ill, aged, or disabled loved ones.

    Web site—www.nfcacares.org

    Phone—1-800-896-3650

National Institute on Aging—conducts research on aging and reports findings to the federal government.

    Web site—www.nia.nih.gov

    Phone—1-800-222-2225

National Organization for Empowering Caregivers—helps provide assistance, education, support, referrals, and volunteers for family caregivers.

    Web site—www.nofec.org

    Phone—(212) 807-1204

Older Women's League—strives to improve the status and quality of life of midlife and older women; accomplishes its work through research, education, and advocacy activities conducted through a chapter network.

    Web site—www.owl-national.org

    Phone—(202) 783-6686 or 1-800-825-3695

Rosalynn Carter Institute for Caregiving—promotes mental health and well-being of individuals, families, and professional caregivers by building public awareness of caregiving needs.

    Web site—www.rci.gsw.edu

    Phone—(229) 928-1234

Senior Law Home Page—provides information to senior citizens, their families, attorneys, social workers, and financial planners about elder law, Medicare, Medicaid, guardianship, estate planning, trusts, and the rights of the elderly and disabled.

    Web site—www.seniorlaw.com

The Sandwich Generation—provides information for those sandwiched between aging parents and younger children.

    Web site—www.sandwichgeneration.com

    Address—P. O. Box 132, Wickatunk, NJ 07765

Publications

Alzheimer's Foundation of America—for caregivers of persons with Alzheimer's disease and related illnesses.

    Web site—www.alzfdn.org

    Phone—1-866-AFA-8484 (1-866-232-8484)

Caring Today—provides practical advice for the family caregiver.

    Web site—www.caringtodaymagazine.com

    Phone—1-800-480-4851

Mature Living—provides information and inspiration to Christian senior adults.
> Web site—www.lifeway.com
> Phone—1-888-841-3401

Today's Caregiver Magazine—America's magazine for family and professional caregivers; provides information, support, and guidance for families and professional caregivers; offers newsletters, online discussion lists, chat rooms, and an online store.
> Web site—www.caregiver.com
> Phone—1-800-829-2734

New Hope® Publishers is a division of WMU®,
an international organization that challenges Christian
believers to understand and be radically involved in
God's mission. For more information about WMU,
go to www.wmu.com. More information
about New Hope books may be found at
www.newhopepublishers.com. New Hope books
may be purchased at your local bookstore.